INDYCAR™

INDYCAR™

Kris Perkins

OSPREY
AUTOMOTIVE

For Sean and Aran

First published in Great Britain in 1993 by Osprey,
an imprint of Reed Consumer Books Limited,
Michelin House, 81 Fulham Road,
London SW3 6RB
and Auckland, Melbourne, Singapore and Toronto

© 1993 Reed International Books Limited

All rights reserved. Apart from any fair dealing for the purpose of private study, research, criticism or review, as permitted under the Copyright, Designs and Patents Act, 1988, no part of this publication may be reproduced, stored in a retrieval system, or transmitted in any form or by any means, electronic, electrical, chemical, mechanical, optical, photocopying, recording. or otherwise, without prior written permission. All enquiries should be addressed to the publisher.

ISBN 1 85532 399 0

Editor Shaun Barrington
Page design Paul Kime/Ward Peacock Partnership
Printed in Hong Kong

Acknowledgements

My thanks go to Jean Wilson and to all the following people who gave their help and support in producing this book.
Roger Bailey, president American Racing Series, Inc; Susan Bradshaw, Marlboro Racing Team Penske; Steve Bunkhall, project manager Lola Cars Ltd; David Elshoff, Championship Auto Racing Teams, Inc; Chip Ganassi, Chip Ganassi Racing; Nick Goozee and staff, Penske Racing; Sandie Graydon, American Racing Series, Inc; Deke Houlgate, Pennzoil Hall/VDS Racing; Gwyneth Hughes, Texaco; Mario Illien, Ilmor Engineering; Michael A Knight, Newman-Haas Racing; Rodger A Lee, vice president Bell Auto Racing Division; Alan Mertens, Galmer Engineering; Paul Morgan, Ilmor Engineering; Vince Muniga, Cadillac; Line Page, Ilmor Engineering, Roger Penske, Penske Racing; Denise Proctor, Cosworth Engineering; Mark Rollinson, Buick Motor Division; Rebecca Sargeant and staff, Galmer Engineering; Dr Susanne J Senhenn; Marc Spiegel, Valvoline; William Stokkan, Championship Auto Racing Teams, Inc; Anna Terry; Derrick J Walker, president Walker Motorsport; Mike Webb; Steve Weiss and staff of Championship Auto Racing Teams, Inc.
No list of acknowledgements would be complete without mentioning Dan R Boyd and Duane Appleget, two fine photographers without whom the majority of the pages in this book would have been white space; and Colorsport Photographic Agency, London. Last, but by no means least, I would like to thank editor Shaun Barrington at Osprey for his help and encouragement.

Front cover
27 Grand Prix and the Formula One World Drivers Championship in 1992. For 1993, a new challenge for Nigel Mansell

Half-title page
Scott Pruett flings his Budweiser Lola into a corner at Surfers Paradise, Australia, at the start of the 1991 IndyCar Series. (Acikalin/Colorsport)

Back cover
Al Unser Jr pit stops during the Indy 500 in 1990. The fuel/air jack operator is wearing full Nomex overalls, gloves, boots and helmet as protection against fire. (David Taylor/Colorsport)

Title page
Michael Andretti began his successful attack on the 1991 Indy Championship at Surfers Paradise, Australia, in his Newman-Haas Lola-Ford-Cosworth, race number 2. (John Fryz/Colorsport)

For a catalogue of all books published by Osprey Automotive
please write to:

**The Marketing Department, Reed Consumer Books,
1st Floor, Michelin House, 81 Fulham Road, London SW3 6RB**

Above
Dutchman Arie Luyendyk at speed in the Target Scotch Video Lola T92/00 Ford Cosworth. (Dan R Boyd/Chip Ganassi Racing)

Contents

Fabrizzio Barbazza lapping the Indianapolis Motor Speedway on 27 May 1987.
(Focus West/Bob Beck/Colorsport)

An introduction to IndyCar racing

For a long time in Europe we have been engrossed with the antics of Formula One racing, which has developed into a highly sophisticated spectacle that attracts thousands to the tracks around the world and millions of spectators at home. In recent years the technical development of the cars has somewhat detracted from the skills of the drivers as a more advanced car will dominate a race rather than providing good close racing through equally matched vehicles. Through this period the British had been somewhat lacking in a national hero until Nigel Mansell began to emerge as a contender for the Formula One crown that was being fiercely defended by an equally determined Ayrton Senna in the Honda powered McLaren.

Eventually Renault and Frank Williams got the recipe right and Nigel Mansell and Ricardo Patrese began to show that the Honda McLaren was no longer the leading light. The races once more became entertaining with tough sometimes controversial disputes taking place on the track. Having come close the previous year Nigel Mansell finally proved his point by winning the 1992 FIA World Championship Formula One title by round 11, having won nine of the 16 Grand Prix and notching up 13 pole positions. But as in so many other activities internal politics and money matters caused disputes within the racing teams and in frustration the new Champion decided that rather than fight off-track he would leave the disputes and tackle new territory.

Having been approached on numerous occasions he finally discussed with Paul Newman and Carl Haas the possibility of entering the IndyCar series, a motorsport event largely unknown in Great Britain or Europe.

One easily forgets that auto racing is not unique to us Europeans and that similar events have been taking place within the United States of America since the early 1900s. Anyone with an interest in motorsport has heard of the Indianapolis 500 but few in Europe know what sort of cars take part or of the legends in the driving seat: Mario Andretti, AJ Foyt, Danny Sullivan, Emerson Fittipaldi, and Rick Mears are just some of

Michael Andretti leads his father Mario Andretti – both are driving Kmart/Havoline 191 Ford Cosworth XB cars. (Dan R Boyd/Newman-Haas)

Left
Pre-season testing at the Firebird Raceway, Phoenix, Arizona for Hall/VDS team driver Teo Fabi in the Pennzoil Special 1993 Lola-Chevy Indy V8/C. (Michael Dunn/Pennzoil)

famous names who take part in the world's fastest, open wheel motorsport.

This book supplies the answers to the questions about the most well known and growing race series – IndyCar racing. In simple terms the differences between the two types of car are as follows: Formula One cars (minimum weight 500 kg) are lighter and therefore more nimble than an IndyCar (minimum weight 705 kg); this is mainly because the latter have to be built more robustly to withstand possible impact with the concrete walls of an oval track at speeds in excess of 200 mph. IndyCars (2.65 – litre V8 as opposed to the 3.5 litre V10 F1) are allowed to be turbocharged, boosting power output slightly above the 750 bhp delivered by higher revving (13,500 rpm) F1 engines; IndyCar powerplants peak at around 11,500 rpm. To keep the cars on the track and enable high speeds the IndyCar has an aerodynamic underside that helps suck the car down onto the track, a feature banned in F1.

An important factor in IndyCar is the restriction on high technology such as expensive automatic gearboxes, traction control devices and 'active' suspension systems, which are all banned in an attempt to keep the teams ultra-competitive. The other significant difference between IndyCar and F1 is in the braking department; carbon fibre disc brakes are the norm on an F1 car but are only allowed in IndyCar racing for Speedway events. Finally, IndyCars are set up with staggered wheels for oval racing and even the steering wheel will be offset to help the driver cope with turns on the banking.

Above

The pressures of team ownership: Paul Newman watches the 'Red Five' of star driver Nigel Mansell from the pit wall. Mansell signed a contract worth a reported $4.5 million to drive for Newman-Haas in the 1993 IndyCar series. (Dan R Boyd)

After his first foray in an IndyCar, on 4 January 1993 at the 1.6 mile Firebird Raceway at Phoenix in Arizona, Nigel Mansell found the 1992 Lola completely different to anything he had driven before and prepared for a steep learning curve. Nevertheless, the F1 World Champion went out and set some very impressive speeds, circulating within half a second of the lap record after only a few minutes. As part of his settling in process he deliberately spun the car to discover how it reacted before taking the necessary corrective actions.

After pitting to change tyres, which were scrubbed out after his spectacular spin tests, Mansell powered back out onto the track. After completing a total of only 35 laps he broke the circuit lap record by one tenth of a second, an impressive drive by any standards.

Another new experience awaited Mansell at the Phoenix International Raceway – an oval track. A few exploratory laps and he was circulating within a half second of the lap record. This performance was watched and enjoyed by a large crowd of media personnel who, at the end of the session – curtailed early due to rain – applauded this demonstration of driving.

A test session was held at Laguna Seca Raceway in California where Mansell broke the lap record before he again returned to the Phoenix International Raceway to try out his new 1993 Lola T9306. After warming up the tyres and getting a feel for the car's handling, he began to build up speed... the result was three new lap records in succession – simply astonishing. But it is one thing to race the stop watch, quite another to compete against top drivers all equally determined to win and with many seasons of IndyCar experience behind them.

The opening round of the 1993 PPG IndyCar World Series Championship was held at Surfers Paradise in Queensland, Australia. In the opening practice session on the 2.793 mile, 16 turn road circuit, Mansell posted warning of his intentions by setting a fast 1 min 40.414 sec lap, but when this was broken by Penske drivers' Emerson Fittipaldi and Paul Tracy something better was obviously required. After some adjustments to the Lola's aerodynamics by Newman-Haas race engineer Peter Gibbons, Mansell went out again and set a new time of 1 min 38.555 secs, earning provisional pole position.

At the start of the race it was rookie Nigel Mansell who led the field, but he made the mistake of getting too close to the pace car and had to brake to avoid shunting its rear. Second place starter Emerson Fittipaldi seized his chance and shot ahead, followed by team mate Paul Tracy with Robby Gordon in the AJ Foyt Lola T92/00-Ford in tow. Mansell's inexperience had cost him the lead and it was lap 16 before 'Red Five' could get past the other cars to take the front. Mansell managed to out brake Emerson Fittipaldi going into Jupiter's Casino Corner at the end of the back straight, but in doing so he had impinged the rules, as yellow flags were being waved at the entrance to the turn to warn of an earlier accident. The manoeuvre had flat spotted Mansell's tyres – as he discovered accelerating down the straight – but at the same time Newman-Haas pit manager Jim McGee called him to pit. For the overtake carried out under the yellow flags Mansell was given an immediate stop 'n' go penalty which, to his great good fortune, happened to coincide with his first pit stop. Returning to the track he took the lead again on lap 22 of the 65 five lap race and looked set for any easy win before a suspected puncture demanded another pit stop which relegated him to fourth place. When the two leading cars, driven by Emerson Fittipaldi and Robby Gordon, made their second scheduled pit stop Mansell regained the lead; despite fuel shortages, a brake pedal digging into the sole of his right foot and increasing fatigue, he drove securely to take the win by 5.113 secs. Second place was taken by Emerson Fittipaldi from hard pressing Robby Gordon and Mansell's team mate Mario Andretti came in fourth.

Mansell's win was at a new race record time of 1 hr 52 min 2.286 secs, an average of 97.284 mph, and was the first victory by a rookie driver since the late Graham Hill's audacious winning debut in 1966 at the Indianapolis 500. Nigel Mansell had made an impressive IndyCar debut but he still had to experience the unique taste of IndyCar racing at an oval track, the first test of which would be the Phoenix International Raceway.

On Saturday 3rd April during practice for the Valvoline 200 race the following day, Nigel Mansell was introduced to the dangers of oval tracks in dramatic fashion. Having warmed up his tyres, Mansell was gradually increasing his speed when he lost the rear end of the car going into Turn One and hit the concrete retaining wall at 185 mph. So hard was the impact that it punched a hole through the wall and triggered a fireflash from fuel, oil and rubber debris. Mansell suffered a blackout and concussion due to the violent deceleration. Although the immense strength of the car prevented further injuries, there was initial concern about swelling in his lower back caused by internal bleeding.

Within hours of being helicoptered to hospital he was sitting up in bed arguing his case to be allowed to go back and drive in the race. However, IndyCar rules clearly state that if a driver is knocked unconscious during practice they are barred from competing in the race.

Questioned afterwards Nigel recalled going into the turn with his foot down on the accelerator but then lost the rear end and had no chance to recover it. One of the many theories put forward for the cause of the crash is that the rear end of the car hit a patch of rubber debris ('marbles'), which broke the grip of the tyres and caused the power to slide the car round. Having been bitten by the dangers of the oval track, Mansell was keen to get 'back in the saddle' and dispel any qualms about his ability to put the experience behind him.

The following day his Newman-Haas team mate Mario Andretti broke a dry spell of 73 races without a win by emerging victorious from a crash-studded Valvoline 200 mile. Canadian Paul Tracy had stormed into a four lap lead when he lost it at speed and crashed into the same wall as Nigel Mansell. A short while later Emerson Fittipaldi – who had taken up the lead after Paul Tracy's incident, crashed at turn four allowing Mario Andretti to take the front, victory, and the lead in the Championship. The 200-mile race was his 377th IndyCar start, an all-time record, and gave him his 52nd win – only the legendary AJ Foyt has more with 67. The event also marked Andretti's 100th major auto racing win, his first with a Ford Cosworth XB engine and, aged 53, he became the oldest ever IndyCar winner. A day to remember...

IndyCar racing is always close; with Nigel Mansell keen to recover his lead in the series the rest of the Championship promised to be entertaining but only time would tell whether he could conquer the ovals.

Mansell now faced what he considered to be the biggest challenge of his driving career, the Indianapolis 500, the glorious month of May: a full month of testing and preparation for the gruelling five-hundred-mile race for which he was still unqualified.

Following the operation on his injured back Mansell was a late arrival to the Indianapolis Speedway and was left with only four days of qualifying time. First of all, he had to pass his Rookie test, where his driving around the 2.5 mile oval would be scrutinised by a panel of drivers and officials, who would decide whether he could race. This test was held on Wednesday the 12th of May. To begin with he was given a tour of the circuit by Mario Andretti who pointed out all the undulations and the new features of the track. After a classroom session where further details of the track were presented, he began his four circuit sessions in the car: ten laps at 180, then 190 and then at 195 mph. The final test was to show that he could maintain control at speeds in excess of 200mph. Did he pass? Take a guess. To prove that he was capable of more, Mansell went out again in a late afternoon session and posted the third fastest speed of the day, 222.77 mph. The only question now was the startling possibility of pole position straight off the bat.

A few days later, 15th of May, Pole Day turned out to be very hot, the track slippery with accumulating oil and rubber. This dictated the results. Mario Andretti went out onto the track at 11.00 am and set a four lap average of 223.414 mph which went unchallenged until late afternoon. Nigel Mansell had one attempt in the heat but figured that the optimum time for his challenge would come later. At around 4.30 Arie Luyendyk,

"the Flying Dutchman", went out onto the track and on his first lap set an attention-grabbing 223.892 mph. His next lap was even faster, 224.316, followed by two consistent laps of 223.830, giving him provisional pole position. Yet there was still the threat of Nigel Mansell and Emerson Fittipaldi to come.

First out was Nigel and on his first lap he ran a 221.811 which was way off the pace – the changes in the track were hindering rather than helping. The next lap was even more disappointing, 219.074, and the next two laps were not spectacular, apart from a high exit from turn four. These times gave an average of 220.255 mph, putting him in eighth place just ahead of Emerson Fittipaldi, who had suffered a similar fate to Nigel.

At the start of the 77th Indianapolis 500, in front of 450,000 spectators – the world's largest sporting event in terms of paid attendance – it was Brazilian Raul Boesel who led into turn one followed by the rest of the pack, including Nigel Mansell whose hopes of stealing a place or two by diving through the inside were thwarted by heavy traffic. At the front Boesel began to pull away from Luyendyk and Mario Andretti with laps of around 214 mph – 10 mph slower than the opening laps the

Indianapolis 500, Sunday, May 30, 1993. As Nigel Mansell was to find out in final qualifiying, the circuit is notorious for its surface changes. The hot, humid conditions made the track very slippery and the new boy could only manage to qualify in eighth place – though previous injury played a part

previous year. The drop in pace was due to the restrictions on car aerodynamics and to the revised track layout. By lap nine the lead cars had closed up on and began passing the slower cars.

At this point there was the first yellow of the race, for Jim Crawford who had spun in Turn Two, which was the signal for most of the lead drivers to make their first pit stop. By lap 32 Mario Andretti was in front and continued to lead the field until lap 46 when Arie Luyendyk took over. Mansell was pacing himself and on lap 70 took the lead before relinquishing the spot to team mate Mario Andretti on lap 91 as he pitted. This, his third stop, was a minor disaster as he over-shot his pit and had to be pushed back, costing valuable time and places. On the track Mario Andretti set the pace and looked as if he was in with a chance of that elusive win but he was given a stop 'n' go penalty, for allegedly entering the pits when they were closed following a shunt between his son Jeff Andretti and Roberto Guerrero. At the re-start on lap 138 Al Unser Jr was in the lead pursued by Mario Andretti, who had been stopped and had re-joined the field still under a yellow flag, followed by Al Unser Sr, Scott Brayton, Emerson Fittipaldi and Nigel Mansell. By lap 174, when the race was re-started after yet another yellow flag, Mario Andretti was leading from Emerson Fittipaldi and Nigel Mansell, who made a successful bid for the lead by diving around the outside as they went into Turn One. Out in front the Englishman looked confident but another yellow flag allowed Emerson Fittipaldi and Arie Luyendyk to close up on him. As the green flag was waved both drivers got the jump on Mansell and Fittipaldi passed on the inside whilst Luyendyk squeezed by on the outside. What's that old phrase about no substitute for experience?

The Brazilian was out in front and pulling away with Mansell in third place. In Turn Two on lap 193 he drifted out too far and hit the wall with both right-hand wheels. Fortunately he recovered and kept going, even though the yellow flags were already being waved for the incident. At the end of lap 195 the green flag was waved again and the cars pushed for the final few laps. Victory went to Emerson Fittipaldi, his second Indy 500, 2.862 seconds ahead of Arie Luyendyk, with Nigel Mansell just three seconds behind him.

One thing about IndyCar racing is that the racing is close – and this was some of the closest ever, with 21 lead changes among 12 drivers. Mansell's third place pushed his points in the championship to 50, giving him the lead overall from Mario Andretti in second on 43. For such a driver, third place was not enough. "I'm still learning. I'm not making any excuses, I just goofed up." It didn't take long for Mansell to conquer the ovals for the first time, with a victory in the next race at the (admittedly very different) Milwaukee circuit.

A brief history of IndyCar racing

The sport of motor racing has been around for over a hundred years. It originated with the very early models built in Europe but the idea soon caught on in the United States of America.

The very first road race in America was organised by the Chicago Herald, held through the streets of Chicago in November 1895, during which competitors reached speeds of up to 7 mph. It was won by J Frank Duryea, whose petrol powered car was lubricated with oil supplied by the new Valvoline company. The following year the first enclosed track event was held at Narragansett Park, Cranston, Rhode Island. Huge crowds, who were charged an entrance fee, flocked to see the competitors race five laps around a one mile dirt track. The race was won surprisingly by A H Whiting's Riker electric powered car which beat the other seven competitors with an average speed of 24 mph. The commercial success of this hugely popular event was to set the pattern of road racing throughout the United States over the following years.

Championship car racing originated in the United States in 1902, when, after a series of different races, the year's best driver was decided upon by the media rather than by the driver winning the most races.

The successful marques in Europe – Renault, Fiat and Mercedes – were imported into the country and soon dominated many events. Public interest in motor racing was growing throughout the world but Britain had fallen behind due to the restrictions on public road racing. Enter Hugh Fortescue Locke-King: he built the world's first purpose-built speedway track at Brooklands in Surrey, England. Opened in 1907, the Brookland Motor Course revolutionised racing car design. To cope with the speeds and banking of the 2.75 mile (4.42 km) concrete track, cars became more aerodynamic and developed cowls at the back to aid stability.

The success of Brooklands soon caught on in the States and in 1908 the Atlanta oval opened; this two mile gravel surfaced track was built by Asa Chandler and Ed Durant.

By 1909 the recently formed American Automobile Association promoted the AAA Championship race series. This consisted of 24 races held during a hectic five month season. Variety was the hallmark of these early races which ranged from short sprints to long distance events such as a race from Los Angeles to Phoenix, Arizona. In August 1909 three races were held at the new Indianapolis oval track but this

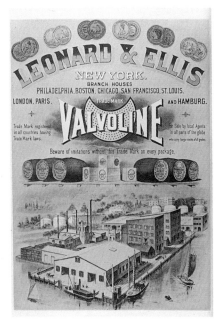

Above
Valvoline have had a long association with motorsport and the IndyCar series. (Valvoline)

Opposite
Racing cars didn't come much larger than Ray Haroun's #32 Marmon Wasp. A feature of this car was the rear view mirror, a vital device as Haroun, unlike other competitors, raced alone and therefore relied upon his mirror to see what was happening on the track behind him. (Duane J Appleget)

first event was horribly marred by the loss of five lives.

The Indianapolis circuit was initially designed by local entrepreneur Call Fisher as a testing ground for automobiles but he soon realised it could also generate money as a venue for the proposed AAA Championship. To help finance the project he brought in three local businessmen named James Allison, Arthur Newby and Frank Wheeler, to form the Indianapolis Motor Speedway Corporation. Their combined capital of $750,000 bought a 320 acre site northwest of the city limits.

A rectangular circuit was rapidly built with slightly banked corners. Using the tarmacadam principle, the track consisted of a crushed rock base covered by asphalt. The track was 2.5 miles in length, composed of a 0.9 mile start and back straights connected by 0.25 mile, 9 ft high banked corners linked by 0.6 mile short straights.

The early cars were not very powerful but weighed a great deal and during the first few races that season they badly damaged the circuit. The track obviously had to be resurfaced with a more durable material. Over three million building bricks were put down during the next 14 months and spectators were provided with covered stands along the straights. Upon completion the venue with its improved surface was ready to stage its first long distance event. The inaugural Indianapolis 500 mile race was held on 30 May 1911. An interested 55,000 crowd watched as the 40 strong field of American, Case, Interstate, National and Simplex cars. together with a liberal sprinkling of European machines, set off after the Stoddard-Dayton Pace car in a cloud of exhaust smoke and dust. Six hours, forty-two minutes and eleven seconds later, having covered five hundred miles, the winner crossed the line. His name was Ray Harroun, driving a six-cylinder Marmon Wasp machine, race number 32. The majority of contestants drove stripped down passenger cars and were accompanied by a mechanic, who also acted as an observer. The race winner had driven on his own to reduce weight that he believed caused tyre wear in the turns. Without the 'riding mechanic' to act as observer he had his machine fitted with a high rear view mirror.

The Marmon Wasp, like most of the machines in the race was very long at the front to accommodate the large 500 cubic inch engine. The massive fuel tank was located immediately behind the drivers seat. These

Well coordinated pit crew action on the Carrick car Rick Mears drove in 1985 while recovering from injury. Later in the year he stepped aside to let Al Unser successfully campaign the IndyCar title. Unser handed over the symbolic number one to Rick Mears for the 1986 season

monsters had large wheels which meant that the cars stood high off the ground. Throughout the race Ray Harroun had averaged a speed of 74.602 mph, which was an impressive performance at the time. During the race Harroun stopped three times for tyres, while other competitors made up to twelve tyre stops, his decision to drive alone obviously paid off.

The race was truly a test of both mechanical and human endurance and was recognised as a valuable publicity medium. Race promoters quickly cashed in and soon there were 24 Speedway tracks, most were wooden board surfaced which were cheap and easy to construct, dotted around the country near the major cities. The crowds were drawn in their thousands to watch the cars speeding around these tracks such as, Sheepshead Bay in Brooklyn, Chicago, Tacoma, Uniontown and Santa Monica. The cars remained pretty much the same in appearance but under their big bonnets the engines became smaller yet more powerful resulting in higher lap speeds. In 1914 Rene Thomas with his Delage, set a One Lap Qualifying speed of 94.54 mph, by 1919 he had raised this speed to 104.78 mph. With the emphasis on speed rather than handling and braking, engine development and aerodynamics took precedence. Supercharging produced enormous amounts of power and attention then turned to reliability.

Over the next few years the oval race series grew in popularity and importance for the motor manufacturers both in the United States and in Europe. Dario Resta dominated the 1915 season with his Peugeot and the following season he duelled with Ralph De Palma and his Mercedes both featuring twin overhead camshaft engines with four valves per cylinder. Another driver achieving notable success with a Peugeot that season was Johnny Aitken.

Great steps forward had been made in engine technology during the war years and these soon manifested themselves in the motor industry. The Championship race series was a great proving ground and advertisement for developments in tyres, supercharging, transmission and suspension systems. One of the leading American engines was that developed by Harry Miller and by 1917 Duesenberg, Frontenac, Peerless and Stutz were also beginning to establish themselves. Through the 1920s Speedway racing continued to develop and became more technically advanced on the engine side than their European rivals, as was reflected in the results. From 1921 the American Automobile Association (AAA) National Championship was dominated by Duesenberg and Miller cars. At the same time the Indianapolis track was recognised as the event of the season with the month of May devoted to a steady build up of events leading to the race on the 30th.

In 1925 Peter DePaulo won the Indianapolis 500 mile race at an

In 1986 Rick Mears became the first driver to earn more than one million dollars in a year ($1,414,472 to be exact), and came fourth in the driver performance chart behind Danny Sullivan, Al Unser Jnr and Bobby Rahal

average speed of over 100 mph with a Miller engined car, but money for the development of racing cars was already beginning to become difficult to find as the sport was so specialised.

Then in 1927 the Indianapolis track was acquired by the famous First World War flying ace, Eddie Rickenbacker, the former number one driver for the Prest-O-Lite, Maxwell racing team. The racing continued but many of the teams were forced through financial reasons to use highly modified but cheaper stock car engines. The Great Depression saw the situation get even worse and a number of the smaller engine manufacturers disappeared. For those who remained, like Miller and Offenhauser, the challenge for more speed went on and in the same year Peter DePaulo raised the One Lap qualifying speed to 120.546 mph. A decade later the speed had risen to 130.492 mph, set by Jimmy Snyder but the race itself was narrowly won by Wilbur Shaw from Ralph Hepburn. A significant factor in the rise in speed must have been made by the laying of asphalt over the bricks in the banked corners during the winter of 1936. Over the next few years further stretches were resurfaced until only a narrow strip of bricks remained across the start/finish line. This 'yard of bricks' remains today as a reminder of 'the Brickyard' track. The last race for some five years was held in 1941 and was won by Mauri Rose and Floyd Davis, whom the former relieved part way through the race. The morning of race day was marked by a huge fire which totally destroyed the old fuel dump area known as 'Gasoline Alley'.

The track remained unused during the war and its surface became badly broken up by weeds. It was then bought and renovated by local businessman Tony Hulman. Thanks to his efforts the Indianapolis 500 race resumed in 1946 when it was won by George Robson.

The importance of the Indianapolis race had a major influence on the rest of the permanent race tracks throughout the country, many of which were still the wooden boarded tracks dating back to before the First World War. To keep pace the rest of the Speedway tracks around the United States had to quickly improve their surfaces and modernise their facilities for both competitors and spectators. Motorsport was once again growing in popularity and attracting increasing numbers of spectators as well as an International media interest.

In the search for more speed IndyCars became lower by reducing the ground clearance and with long sleek bonnets that housed tremendously powerful engines. The domination of the series by Miller engines was ended by Offenhauser, or 'Offy' engines and these were to power numerous championship winners during the following years.

At this time the races in America were extremely popular but despite this received little interest from foreign drivers until in 1950, in an attempt to attract European drivers and manufacturers, the Indianapolis 500 was included in a new championship, the Formula One World Championship. This new series of seven races organised by the Federation Internationale L'Automobile began with the first race at Silverstone on the 13th of May which was won by Giuseppe Farina of Italy with an Alfa Romeo. A few weeks later on its customary date of the 30th of May the third round of the Formula One World Championship was held. Another attempt to boost IndyCar racing abroad was made in 1957 when an IndyCar 500 mile race was held at the steeply banked Monza circuit in Italy. Unfortunately the hoped for interest from Europe did not materialise and the race, which was stopped after 345 miles due to bad weather, was won by Johnny Parsons in his Wynn's Friction Proof sponsored Offenhauser/Kurtis. The next few years saw very few European drivers venture over the Atlantic to contest this round and in turn few American drivers went over to race in Europe.

Almost without exception all the IndyCars at this time had forward mounted engines with rear-wheel drive. Yet in Europe experiments were being carried out on the race circuits with rear engined machines. In 1961 the beginning of the end of the front engine IndyCar was heralded by the appearance of Jack Brabham's rear engined lightweight modified

Rick Mears in the Pennzoil Penske machine; he was part of a three car Penske operation with Danny Sullivan and Emerson Fittipaldi

Formula One Cooper race car. At the Indy 500 it caused a sensation by finishing ninth. Two years later the Milwaukee 200 mile race was won by a rear mounted Ford-Lotus powered car driven by Scotsman, Jim Clark. He went on to win the Indianapolis 500 in 1965 and set the trend for IndyCars during the 70s. Amongst the famous drivers of this decade were A J Foyt, Jim Clark, Graham Hill and Mario Andretti. Some of these had made their reputations on the European and World championship circuits but successfully transferred to the rigours of Indy racing.

Turbocharging of engines had become increasingly necessary as a means of boosting power outputs to raise speeds. In 1962 Parnelli Jones broke the 150 mph qualifying speed record, this was then raised to 160.973 mph in 1965 by Jim Clark in a Ford-Lotus and up to 171.887 mph in 1968 by Graham Hill. Gas turbine powered cars made a brief appearance in 1967 and again in 1968 before they were banned.

Attention then turned to European engine manufacturers such as Cosworth Engineering and their highly successful DFV (Double Four Valve) engine. In 1972 the One Lap Qualifying speed was raised to 196.678 mph by Bobby Unser driving an Offenhauser. His father Al Unser Senior in search of more power turned to a Cosworth DFX engine, with which he won the race in 1978. The Cosworth engine was to dominate the Indy championship for the following decade before it in turn was superseded by Chevrolet engines. With race speeds continuing to rise numerous attempts were made by the AAA to slow the cars down by introducing rules limiting engine size, minimum weights, fuel restrictions, etc. But where there's a will there's a way and in 1977 Tom Sneva broke the 200 miles per hour mark with his Cosworth during qualifying. In 1984, again with a Cosworth engine he increased the speed to 210.689 mph but the race was won by Rick Mears in a Chevrolet at an awesome 220.453 mph.

Between 1978 and 1987 Cosworth dominated the most prestigious event in the motorsport calendar, the Indianapolis 500, by winning on ten consecutive occasions. This victorious period was both started and finished by Al Unser.

In 1978 IndyCars made their appearance in Great Britain at Silverstone on 30th September and Brands Hatch on 7th October. The visit was marked by the short course at Brands Hatch being named, the Indy circuit. Another milestone of the 70s was the first woman to compete in IndyCar racing: Janet Guthrie entered the Trenton 200 race in 1976 and came fifteenth. The following year she became the first woman to compete in the Indianapolis 500 where she completed 27 laps to finish 29th.

It is a fact of most sports that some form of politics develops and IndyCars were not exempt. From the very beginning in 1909 until 1955

An unidentified driver poses in his 1940s racing car, a Stevens-Winfield 3/C, sponsored by guess who?

C Yarborough smiling for the cameras before the start of the 1967 Indy 500, which was won by the remarkable A J Foyt in a rear-engined Coyote Ford

the season long championship had been run by the AAA but from 1956 until 1979 the United States Auto Cub (USAC) governed the sport. But many drivers and race car owners felt that they should have a say in the rule making and administration of their sport. Therefore in 1978 they launched their own governing body, Championship Auto Racing Teams, Inc. (CART), headed by Roger Penske and U E Patrick. The principles of CART were to promote the sport as a form of entertainment, and give greater support to the drivers, their sponsors and the promoters. With radical differences in opinion on the way the sport should be run the rift between the USAC and CART steadily grew so that events began to be organised separately.

The first CART organised event was the 150 mile race at Phoenix International Raceway in Arizona on 11 March 1979. The race, won by Gordon Johncock was televised by NBC. This success resulted in USAC retaliating by refusing the entries of the CART teams into that year's Indianapolis 500, a move that was overturned in court. Moves to reconcile the two bodies saw the formation of a united organisation, CRL, Championship Racing League. But further disputes continued at the start of the following season and any hope of unity evaporated so CART assumed responsibility for the rest of the series.

The sport thrived on the increased media interest and in 1980 PPG Industries, impressed by what they had seen announced that they would sponsor that seasons racing. This sponsorship deal made the CART series the richest in motor racing history, the Indianapolis 500 being the premier event. Not surprisingly the series attracted even more television coverage, NBC televised the whole of the Michigan 500 race won by Pancho Carter live. With live television a huge audience was made available – to prospective sponsors the situation was ideal for the promotion of their product. Over the following years the television audience has grown to be millions world wide.

The growing interest in the series from abroad led to the first overseas event being held as part of the championship in 1991 at Surfers Paradise, Australia. The race was won by John Andretti, the nephew of world famous Mario Andretti, driving a Hall-VDS car in the team's very first appearance.

1992 saw a change in the race series title, INDYCAR became the official acronym of the world's major motor sport event the PPG IndyCar World Championship. Last year also marked the tenth year of televised action from the race series being broadcast nationally and internationally. IndyCar racing has grown dramatically in popularity and now has a cumulative worldwide television audience of over a quarter of a billion people.

British involvement in IndyCar racing has been dominant for a number of years. The winner of the 1992 IndyCar championship was Bobby Rahal, the first owner/driver since A J Foyt took the title in 1975 and achieved in his very first year in the dual role. He owed much of his success to a number of British firms. His chassis was built by Lola Cars Ltd of Huntingdon in Cambridgeshire and his Chevrolet-Ilmor engine was built by Ilmor Engineering Ltd of Brixworth in Northamptonshire.

Michael Andretti, son of and team mate to Mario Andretti, was runner-up in the championship to Bobby Rahal and established himself as the third highest championship lap leader. He led an amazing 54 per cent of all the laps raced during the season. During the 1992 season he scored 17 of the 31 bonus points available to pole qualifiers and lap leaders. In the final round of the 1992 PPG IndyCar championship at Leguna Seca Raceway at Monterey in California he became the most successful driver of the season with his fifth win, having led all 84 laps and beaten his father into second place. This victory for the Kmart/Havoline Newman-Haas race team was witnessed by the new Formula One World champion Nigel Mansell, who would be taking Michael's place in the team for the 1993 PPG IndyCar World Championship season.

Another star of the 1992 was Al Unser Jr, who was the only driver to score points in all sixteen rounds, the first to do so since Rick Mears back in 1979. In addition he also completed an amazing 99 per cent of the scheduled 2110 laps and 3630 miles of the 3658 miles constituting the season. At Indianapolis the first woman since Janet Guthrie, Lynn St James, qualified for the 500 race in the Agency Rent-A-Car/J C Penney 'Spirit of American Woman' Lola Chevy and finished in an impressive eleventh place.

Competition in IndyCar is not restricted to the drivers, the top four finishers of the 1992 season emphasised the competitive nature favoured by IndyCar with each using a different chassis/engine combination. There were three different chassis and three different engine combinations; Bobby Rahal with a Lola-Chevy Indy V8A-B, Michael Andretti with a Lola-Ford Cosworth XB, Al Unser Jr using a Galmer – Chevy Indy V8A-B, and Emerson Fittipaldi driving a Penske Chevy Indy V8A-B.

The future looks just as exciting with the announcements from two of the major Japanese manufacturers of their intention to enter the IndyCar World series in the near future. Nissan's San Diego, United States based subsidiary, Nissan Performance Technology Inc. (NPTI) announced at the end of 1992 that they were moving into the IndyCar series with a Nissan-powered Lola chassis. The car was initially earmarked for Englishman, Geoff Brabham, son of the former three times Formula One World Champion, Jack Brabham. No stranger to the IndyCar series Brabham has been a regular competitor for seven years

Right
*John Andretti driving the Pennzoil 91
Lola in road trim. The large front wings
create down force for greater track
adhesion*

Right
*John Andretti driving the Pennzoil 91
Lola in road trim. The large front wings
create down force for greater track
adhesion*

with six second places to his credit. Honda too were looking to the future and announced their intention to enter IndyCar racing. They would enter the series in 1994 through their American subsidiary, Acura. They may begin the venture with Bobby Rahal and his Rahal-Hogan Race Team, as the 1992 champion happens to be a major Acura dealer.

To ensure continued competition within the series CART inc. ruled that any new engine manufacturer coming into the PPG IndyCar competition must supply two teams and a minimum of three cars.

If the 1992 season produced such a competitive competition the arrival of the latest Formula One World Champion, Nigel Mansell into IndyCar the series looks to become even more entertaining in the future, possibly 'the most-watched motorsport series in the world'. Mansell viewed his entry into IndyCar as the start of a new career, which is not surprising considering what he would have to contend with. His IndyCar had a manual clutch, a manual gearbox, a turbocharged engine, with its boost control button and the demands of maintaining higher speeds through the turns. According to Nigel Mansell himself, 'The Indy 500 is the biggest challenge to a driver anywhere in the world.'

Rules guide

As in other motor sports the rules and regulations are there to improve safety. The following gives a brief outline of the regulations applying to IndyCars.

Drivers
Licence requirements
All IndyCar competitors must have a valid Federation Internationale de L'Automobile (FIA) Grade A or higher licence and any driver applying for a CART racing licence may have to prove their physical and psychological fitness to participate. There is no definition as to whether you have to be sane or insane to race IndyCars!

The drivers need to be incredibly fit to cope with the stresses imposed upon them during racing. On oval tracks going through the turns the drivers are subjected to 2.5 to 3 times the force of gravity, which imposes a tremendous strain upon the body. In effect a driver weighing 180 lbs will feel as if they weigh over 540 lbs. Therefore all the drivers have to be tremenduously fit to be competitive under the stresses they are subjected to.

For 500 mile events new 'Rookie' drivers may in addition have to pass a driver's test conducted by CART officials.

Clothing
As in most other motorsport fire is the big danger and therefore all drivers must use Nomex™ or Proban™ fire resistant race suits, boots and gloves, with flame retardant underwear, balaclavas and socks. This material is vital but does retain body heat, which means that the driver is often subjected to heat exhaustion if the air temperature and sunlight are high during the race.

Helmet
Every driver has to wear an approved type of safety helmet but the choice of manufacturer is down to the individual. Each helmet is made with fire resistant materials and fitted with a life-support system. This gives the driver an independent air-supply in the event of an accident.

Great attention goes into the manufacture of the helmet shell to help reduce buffeting, which the driver will be subjected to at high speed. Many of the helmets feature slots or other types of spoiler to reduce the buffeting and lifting caused by the low-pressure effect created by the air movement around the car. At high racing speeds, the shape of a

Above
Designed to reduce lift and minimise wind buffeting, this shot clearly shows the slots and vortex generators incorporated into the helmet of John Andretti. (Rodger A Lee/Bell Helmets)

helmet from the face port over the top and to the rear acts like an aircraft wing, creating lift. The spoilers break up the airflow from the curved helmet surface resulting in less helmet lift. Due to the complex airflow dynamics around the helmet and cockpit area, IndyCar drivers experience increasing lateral buffeting as the speed increases.

Thanks to wind tunnel and track testing the manufacturers have now developed vortex generators on the sides of the latest helmets which help in reducing the buffeting. This is achieved by breaking the air away from the helmet surface in a controlled fashion while maintaining a balanced effect.

Kevlar/glassfibre and carbon fibre composites are now the most popular shell materials as they reduce helmet weight without reducing their strength, which can adversely affect the driver's performance under G force while cornering.

Many driver's helmets have a ring, usually fastened to the lower left hand side of the shell, to which a strap can be attached to help reduce the buffeting and give support in the turns.

There are no restrictions on the colour or design of a helmet but the name of the driver must be clearly displayed on each side.

To help reduce the fatigue caused by the strain imposed upon the drivers neck muscles the cars are often fitted with a neck support known as a 'pussy pillow'.

Above
Helmets are carefully designed to limit the often violent head movements associated with driving a car at well over 200 mph, especially on oval circuits; note the ring to attach a support strap. (Rodger A Lee/Bell Helmets)

Right
The cockpit of Rick Mear's Marlboro Penske Chevy 92 – a snug fit. The 'office' of every car is tailored to an individual driver with the seat moulded to the body form, just as in Formula One

The car

To protect the driver the car is of course made as safe as possible, the sidepods which house the radiators, oil coolers and engine management systems, etc are designed to absorb impacts.

The cockpit, 'captains chair' has a minimum opening of 30 × 14 ¾ inches. This individually formed tub must be constructed in carbon fibre, creating a safety shell or 'survival cell' around the driver. The cockpit is such a close fit for the driver that the quick release steering wheel has to be first removed for them to get in or out of the car. The individually moulded seat supports the driver in a reclining position into which they are held by their quick release safety harness of shoulder straps, lap belt and 'anti-submarine' straps.

All the surfaces around the driver's helmet must be smooth and continuous.

Driver instrumentation is made to give clear readings of all critical car and engine functions and therefore features hi-tech digital displays. The instrumentation will usually include the following, some of which are mandatory: ignition switch, engine rpm display, engine temperature, oil temperature, oil pressure and turbocharger boost displays. There will also be a turbocharger boost control, and brake bias control which allows the driver to adjust the braking force bias on the front or rear wheels depending upon race conditions. Also included are a sway bar control for the front and rear, a fire extinguisher release, a low fuel warning light, engine kill switch and a radio mike switch.

To enable ease of use and speed up response several of the switches are located on the steering wheel itself. On the left is a switch for the all important two-way radio link to the pits and the race team manager, while on the right-hand-side of the steering wheel is a switch that if moved to the left jacks up the rear right by an extra 50 lbs of pressure cross weight; moving the switch to the right decreases the pressure on the left.

This ability to alter the bias of the car is of great importance during oval course events.

The cockpit screen or visor must be carefully designed to give the driver maximum protection and an unimpaired view of the track; the height of these will vary from track to track as the driver decides. Bearing in mind that the screen must also keep as much of the wind pressure off the driver as possible, within the constraints of aerodynamics, achieved by the angle of the screen.

The roll-over loop, designed to protect the driver if the car turns over or has an impact at the rear, must extend a minimum of five inches above the drivers helmeted head while they are correctly seated in the car.

Right

The IndyCar revealed, in this case
Al Unser Jr's Chevy V8/B engined Galmer
1. Front wing
2. Shock absorber
3. Vented iron disc
4. Forward rollover hoop bulkhead
5. Manifold pressure relief valve
6. Chevrolet Indy V8 engine
7. Brake cooling air duct
8. Sidepod
9. Carbon fibre tub
10. Roll over hoop
11. Rear suspension shock absorber
12. Rear wing aerofoil

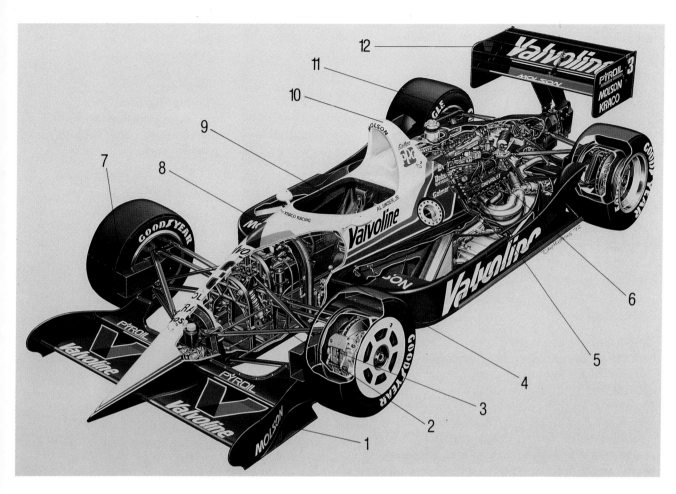

Left
The cockpit of Nigel Mansell's Lola Ford showing the Momo steering wheel and digital Black Box liquid crystal display; just visible on the right hand side is the red knob of the gear lever. (Newman-Haas)

For the 1993 season the cars have been extended at the front to give greater protection to the driver's feet in the event of an accident.

All IndyCars are fitted with on-board automatic/manual fire extinguishers to reduce the fire hazard. One should be securely mounted within the chassis but separated from the driver by a bulkhead with its jets directed at likely fire sources. The areas most prone to fires are around the oil-coolers, exhaust and fuel systems. In addition each car must have a port or ports in the top or side cover of the engine for external extinguisher application.

The cars must be no longer than 195 inches in length with a minimum wheelbase (this is the distance measured between the centre-lines of the front and rear wheels), of 96 inches. Most of the current IndyCars have a wheelbase of between 109 and 113 inches. Their width is restricted to a maximum of 78.5 inches as measured at the rear wheel

Left
The cars are thoroughly checked at the end of every race. The stresses do not merely affect the engine: the chassis endures tremendous forces during braking, accelerating and cornering. Cross-checked measurements taken after the race may indicate new design avenues

outer rim and through the hub centre. Forward of this line the width of the bodywork and all aerodynamic devices is limited to a maximum of 63 inches. Their height, excluding the mandatory roll-over bar, is restricted to 32 inches. The rear wings fitted to add maximum 'downforce' on short ovals and road courses are restricted to a maximum height of 36 inches but limited to 32 inches on Super Speedways or similar fast circuits.

The weight of a turbocharged car must reach a minimum unfuelled weight limit of 1550 lb including coolant and lubricants, the limit for a non-turbocharged car is 1475 lb.

Aerodynamics

The wings fitted to an IndyCar play a vital role in the handling and stability of the car at the high speeds that they are capable of reaching. They also ensure that the power from the engine is fully transferred by maintaining maximum tyre adhesion on the track and help to keep the car balanced.

The aerodynamic requirements vary with the type of track and this will determine the construction of the wings themselves. One element will be used for Superspeedway with as many as five elements forming the wing for a short oval or road course. Because they play such a crucial role long hours and vast sums of money are spent on experimenting in wind tunnels with the form and positioning of both the front as well as the rear wings. The downforce generated by the wings,

Below
From CAD drawings scale models are made for testing in a windtunnel to ensure optimum aerodynamic performance

Above

*A detailed model of the proposed
Galmer 93 car used for wind tunnel
testing. (Galmer)*

which weigh around 20 lb, may be as much as three times the weight of
the car, (around 4500 lb) enabling high speeds to be maintained through
the corners. Because the conditions at the tracks are so variable a great
deal of time is spent setting the wings to obtain the optimum downforce
without creating speed robbing drag.

During a race the front wing elements can be quickly adjusted at a
pit stop by winding attached adjusters, which if the car is understeering
will be turned up or, alternatively, lowered if there is too much
oversteer.

Another factor is that of ground effect. The car's aerodynamics
channel fast flowing air underneath them to create a low pressure effect,
literally sucking the car onto the track. An application of Bernoulli's Law,
that the pressure of a gas falls as its velocity increases. The faster the
airflow the greater the suction, so great care is taken to make the

Above left
*Mario Andretti in action at Phoenix,
Arizona, in the Valvoline 200 race.
During practice he set a new record,
lapping in 20.952 seconds at an
average speed of 171.825 mph*

Left
*Arie Luyendyk, 'The Flying Dutchman',
driving the Target/Scotch Lola Ford
Cosworth at the 1992 Indy 500*

Above
*Michael Andretti in action at the Molson
Indy event in Toronto, Canada. Bobby
Rahal fought hard from the start, but
Andretti was not to be denied and took
the chequered flag to record his third
win of the 1992 season*

underside of the car as smooth as possible apart from the in-built aerofoils.

So effective have aerodynamics become that for 1993 USAC have decided that the aerodynamic devices, vertical 'fences' or 'splitters' that have been developed to increase the ground effect, would be disallowed. This measure, coupled with a 30 per cent reduction of rear wing size on oval tracks, from 17.25 to 12 ft, decreased downforce by around 100 lb. With the reduced downforce top speed on the faster tracks is reduced by around 5 mph.

Chassis

The chassis (or tub) of an IndyCar is a composite construction of aluminium honeycomb and/or carbon fibre with the outer shell or 'skin' formed from carbon fibre, glass fibre or aluminium. Chassis are manufactured by a small number of companies such as Penske Cars Ltd, Lola Cars Ltd, March, Galmer Engineering Ltd, all of which are based, surprisingly, in the United Kingdom. The Rahal-Hogan RCG is the only chassis currently manufactured in the United States.

The chassis themselves are designed on the very latest CAD/CAM equipment using the CART regulations, wind tunnel and data from

Left
The Ford-Cosworth XB IndyCar engine as used by five teams, including Newman-Haas, in 1993. The XB engines are smaller and lighter but more powerful than the earlier DFS IndyCar engines which won 81 races between 1981 and 1986. The XB powerplant developed by Mike Costin and Keith Duckworth promises even greater success. (Cosworth)

previous chassis. These machines can be linked to numerically controlled multi-axis router machines which are used to build fine detailed 1:3 scale models in a very short period of time.

These models are then tested in extraordinarily expensive high speed, moving-ground wind tunnels for aerodynamic evaluation and to determine engine cooling efficiency. Minor modifications are carried out step-by-step so their effects can be analysed and if beneficial accepted into the final package.

Once finalised the model is transferred to full-size bodywork and chassis patterns for hand-finishing and assembly. These pieces then form masters for precision moulds to be made for the carbon fibre composites. The individual pieces are then made up and cured in sophisticated autoclaves.

The rest of the car's components – engines, suspension, transmission and brakes are manufactured, tested and finished at around the same time.

The first prototype will usually be completed around Christmas time ready for immediate track testing in the New Year; the struggle for enhanced perfomance is ceaseless.

If this proves satisfactory full production of the cars begins with the cars being built in pairs and delivery to the customers taking place in late January and early February.

At present a new Lola chassis, as used by Newman-Haas, retails for around $350,000.

Right
The Chevrolet Indy V8/A and V8/B type engines designed by the highly respected Mario Ilien and built by Ilmor Engineering under the direction of Ilien and partner Paul Morgan. Ilmor Engineering was established in January 1984 with financial backing from Roger Penske. The raison d'être of the new concern was IndyCar. Its first engine made its debut in 1986 in a Penske car at Pheonix. The 1991 season record was remarkable: 17 out of 17 pole positions and 17 out of 17 race wins. The even more compact V8/C was campaigned in 1993. (Ilmor)

Engine

The IndyCars use a wide range of manufacturers four-stroke engines, which are usually turbocharged, with a maximum of eight cylinders.

CART issues two kinds of specifications: one for the purpose-built Indy engines and the other for stock block engines. These are engines developed from production car engines, the popular type being the Buick V6. The very strict rules limit the purpose built engines capacity or displacement to a maximum of 2650 cc (161.703 cubic inch in the United States) or 2.65 litres. The turbocharger used must be of a certain size and type with no intercooler allowed.

But for turbocharged engines developed from production, single non-overhead camshaft units, with push rod operated valve operation, like the Buick V6, the capacity rises to a maximum 3430 cc (209.3 ci). Each engine is fitted with a mandatory, Manifold Pressure Relief Valve (Pop-Off valve). These are fitted each day by a CART official and are then collected immediately after each days proceedings. They are a simple but an effective device in limiting the intake manifold pressure to a maximum of 45 inches of mercury or 50 inches for a Buick V6 engine. At Indianapolis, which is outside of USAC control, the Buick turbocharged engines were allowed 55 inches of boost. For 1993 these engines were allowed 52 inches of boost but still remained uncompetitive against the larger, more powerful V8 engines.

If the pressure rises above this limit the valve automatically opens releasing the pressure, the engine revs drop, losing power until the valve

shuts. Every driver tries to ensure that they do not push their engines into operating the valve as the temporary drop in power could easily cost them their place in the race.

Drive is limited to two-wheel-drive either front or rear drive but the majority of current cars use rear drive to push the cars. Most of the engines are set up and controlled using highly sophisticated electronic management systems, individually programmed for each track.

In recent years the engine manufacturers have included, Alfa Romeo (Italy), Buick (USA), Cheverolet (USA), Ford Cosworth (USA/UK), Ilmor Chevrolet (UK/USA), Judd (Japan/UK), and Porsche (Germany), while other manufacturers such as Honda and Nissan plan to enter the sport in the near future.

The engines have dry sump lubrication which means that the three to five gallons of engine oil are not carried in the sump but must be

Above
Frenzied pit crew action on Danny Sullivan's Galmer car during the crash dominated 76th Indianapolis 500 race on 24 May 1992, in which he finished a creditable fifth. (Dan R Boyd)

Above
A 'splash and dash' for Paul Tracy. The Canadian made a tremendous start to the 1993 Championship. (Marlboro)

pumped under pressure from an oil tank to the engine and oil cooling systems.

No oil may be added to the car once it has started a race.

Power output
The power output figures of the engines are measured in horsepower but specific figures for individual cars are very closely guarded secrets but engines usually develop somewhere between 700 and 800 hp.

Turbocharging
To boost the output of the engine and improve its efficiency most engines are turbocharged. The exhaust gasses are directed through the turbocharger where they spin a turbine that compresses and forces the incoming air into the intake manifold. Therefore the engine ingests more

air than if it were normally aspirated. The pressure at which the turbocharger forces the air into the engine is called the 'boost pressure' and is controlled by the 'pressure relief valve'. The increased airflow allows more fuel to be burnt by the engine to increase the power output.

Fuel

IndyCars use a more environmentally friendly fuel than the volatile mixtures used in Formula One car racing. They use alcohol-based methanol fuel, which is composed of oxygen, hydrogen and carbon, commercially made by heating pressurised hydrogen with carbon monoxide. Methanol is considered a renewable resource as it can be made from a variety of natural materials, including processed household refuse. It was chosen for IndyCar use as it has a high octane rating, good combustion burn rate, evaporates quickly and uses less oxygen than a petroleum based fuel. It also has a higher flash point than petrol and is therefore less likely to ignite if spilt on a hot engine. A safety problem with methanol is that it burns with a clear flame making it difficult to spot a fire, although it can be extinguished with water.

Fuel consumption is strictly limited to a minimum of 1.8 mpg as each team is allocated 280 gallons of fuel and the car has a maximum fuel capacity of 40 gallons. The pit tank will hold 240 gallons and at the start of the race the car will be fully fuelled. Methanol does not however produce as much energy as petroleum based fuels. The fuel is carried in a puncture resistant rubber fuel cell, developed by Goodyear, located behind the driver, an area considered least vulnerable. The fuel cells were developed for use in helicopters during the Vietnam war and are made of military standard 30-gauge gum rubber and two plies of 24 ounce rubber impregnated nylon fabric.

As fuel consumption is so important to success or failure, sophisticated computerised engine/fuel management systems are used to ensure that the car has sufficient fuel to complete the race at the fastest pace. The fuel management system will control the precise amount of fuel delivered to each cylinder dependant upon input parameters measured continuously by sensors placed around the engine. These include measurement of the boost pressure, the air inlet temperature and density, throttle position, engine speed, water temperature and fuel pressure. The signals from the sensors are continuously monitored by the computer which interprets and determines the fuel requirements of each cylinder. This process takes place so quickly, in milli-seconds, that it can carry out the operation for each cylinder as it fires.

The engine management system also serves as an operational performance recorder; additional sensors can be added to monitor

Above left
The Buick V6 with which Roberto Guerro gained pole position at the 1992 Indy 500 with a qualifying four lap average speed of 232.482 mph, thus becoming the first driver to break the 230 mph barrier during practice. So far, so good. But on race day Guerro was less than fortunate – he lost control of the car going in to the second turn on the parade lap while warming up his tyres, the resultant impact with the wall putting him out of the running. The Buick V6 Indy engine was a popular powerplant with many teams, but the company withdrew its official sponsorship of the IndyCar series to concentrate on the Firestone Indy Lights racing programme. (Duane J Appleget)

Left
A final check of Michael Andretti's tyres, all of which are carefully marked to ensure correct fitment. (Duane J Appleget)

Roberto Guerro's pit crew practice on race day morning before the 1992 Indy 500. Hopes were high as Roberto had set the qualifying lap record of 232.618 for pole position. On the parade lap when warming up his tyres, he gave it too much, spinning out of the second turn and hitting the wall – which meant instant relegation to 33rd place! (Duane J Appleget)

performance of other car units, so that the continuous logging allows for fault diagnosis and valuable information for development.

Data collected by the electronic management system cannot be down loaded during a race.

On-board camera

Every IndyCar must have a suitable provision for the easy installation of an on-board television camera, which will be mounted at the discretion of CART officials, and its microwave transmitter.

Tyres

All the IndyCars use American Goodyear Racing Eagle radial tyres exclusively. The wheels upon which they are fitted must have a minimum rim diameter of 15 inches, the front wheel width set at ten inches and the rear wheel set at 14 inches. All four of the wheels have a mandatory hub locking device to prevent wheels flying off. The tyres weigh between 18 and 28 lb each depending upon whether its a heavier slick or a lighter wet weather tyre. The tyres at a cost of around $1000 a set of four. A stipulation is that after each race all used tyres must be returned to Goodyear for evaluation. Although everyone is on the same make of tyre there are a range of different compounds usually available and making the correct choice can win or lose a race.

On oval tracks it is standard practice for the cars to be fitted with tyres that have a slightly higher diameter on the outside to help give more control in the turns. The stagger that is usually adopted for on mile ovals is for the outside, right hand tyre to be 3/10 of an inch larger than the left; on road courses zero stagger is used.

After a car has successfully qualified its tyres are removed and impounded until race day when the car must start the race on the same tyres.

To raise the car off the ground during pit stops for tyre changes there are on-board air jacks which are automatically operated by a high pressure air line attached by the vent/jack crew member.

Numbering system

For easy recognition each car must clearly display a race number at the front, on each side and to the back on the rear wing as well as its sides.

The number one plate is awarded to the PPG IndyCar World Series Champion driver for all IndyCar events during the following season. The next numbers, up to twelve are awarded according to the drivers points standing at the end of the preceding season. The number 13 is not used and fourteen belongs to A J Foyt or a car entered by him. This honour was granted in recognition of the driver's long standing performance in IndyCar racing. All other numbers are applied for by the teams and once designated they are used throughout that season.

Running lights

For road course events each car must be fitted with a red rear warning light mounted at the centre point clearly visible to the rear.

Points

Points awarded toward the PPG IndyCar Championship are awarded as follows.

1st	20 points	7th	6 points
2nd	16	8th	5
3rd	14	9th	4
4th	12	10th	3
5th	10	11th	2
6th	8	12th	1

An additional point is awarded to the driver leading a race for the most laps and another point is awarded to the fastest qualifier.

Pre-race qualifying

For oval track events qualifying is carried out in an order dictated by a draw and grid positions set by the fastest of two laps.

In road events the fastest qualifiers from the previous race have individual allocated times during day one, of two days of qualifying, in which to set their fastest lap. The second day groups are set by the fastest and slowest qualifiers with grid positions determined from these sessions. Even if their speeds are higher than earlier qualifiers the later qualifiers take grid positions behind the rest.

Before making a qualifying attempt each driver is given two warm-up laps and the pit crew must green flag signal race officials to warn them that a qualifying attempt is being made. If either the driver or the crew decide to abort the attempt the pit crew can 'wave off' by signalling the race officials with a yellow flag before the driver crosses the finish line of their fourth lap. Once 'waved off' the car must go to the end of the qualifying line up of cars.

Pit regulations

The pit area is extremely dangerous: the competitors enter and leave the area at very high speeds with the added hazard of fuel, pre-occupied mechanics, etc.

Apart from the driver only six crew members are allowed to work on the car in the track pit area. During a race if a car overshoots its designated pit area by more than one pit length the driver must go round With a slight overshoot the car may be pushed back to its area if it does not cause a danger. Penalties are also imposed upon a driver putting any wheel over a fuel or airline hose when entering or leaving the pit area. Usual penalty is a one lap reduction for the offending driver. It is also forbidden to exceed 80 mph having entered the pit lane – ten second stop/go penalty – no limit, of course, when leaving!

Rain

In the interests of safety no oval track event is run if the surface is wet. For road course events when weather conditions are uncertain if the Chief Steward has declared the race a 'dry start' the driver may choose to start on slicks or wet tyres. But if the race is declared a 'wet start' ALL drivers must start on wet weather tyres. If the track conditions change after the start drivers may make their own choice of tyre.

Lights

With the high speeds involved control of the race is maintained by a series of lights that are located around the track or circuit.

A yellow light is shown for any incident that might cause a danger to the drivers and once it is displayed the pace car goes out onto the track. The leader and the following cars will form up behind the pace car

Below
A USAC official checks the pop-off valve on Al Unser Jr's car before the start of the race. (Duane J Appleget)

Flags

A series of different coloured flag signals are used in IndyCar to communicate information to the driver, they are green, blue with a diagonal orange stripe, black, yellow, red, white with a red diagonal stripe, white and a chequered flag. Some will be displayed at the starters station with others being displayed at flag stations located around the race circuit.

Green flag

The green is an 'all-clear' signal which is shown at the start of a practice or qualifying session, it is also shown at the start of a qualifying attempt, the start or re-start of a race on an oval track.

Blue with a diagonal orange stripe flag

This is the 'passing' flag, which when displayed on the approach signifies to the driver that he or she should be prepared to be overtaken.

Black flag

A driver who is shown the black flag must return to the pit area immediately. It may be used to pull off a driver who has a fault with their car or for any infringement of the driving rules.

Yellow flag

When the yellow 'danger' flag is displayed all drivers must slow down, take added care and maintain their positions in the traffic. No overtaking is allowed under direction of a yellow flag. Drivers must travel at a suitable speed while the rest of the field form up behind. If the officials decide that it is necessary a pace car will go out onto the track to lead and therefore regulate the speed of the pack.

On road courses the yellow flag is also used at flag stations to indicate areas of danger, if waved there is greater danger and the driver must reduce speed and be prepared to stop.

Red flag

As soon as the red flag is displayed the race is stopped and all drivers must return slowly to their pit area. If the pit area is closed the drivers must line their cars up in single line along the side of the track wherever the race stewards direct them.

White flag with a red diagonal stripe

Display of this flag from the starter's position indicates to the drivers that an emergency or service vehicle is on the track and that they should reduce speed and exercise extreme caution.

White flag

This flag is shown at the starter's position and informs drivers that they are on their last lap. At road course races a white flag will be waved at a flag station to indicate that an emergency service vehicle is on the track in the next section of the course and that drivers should be cautious on the approach or when passing these vehicles.

Chequered flag

The chequered flag is shown at the end of the race to the winner and to the following cars. During practice or a qualifying session the chequered flag will be shown to signify the end of that period. In addition to flags lights may also be used to supplement certain of the signals.

Pace car

While a yellow flag is displayed around the course a special vehicle, known as the 'pace car' goes out and leads the race leader around the track. The choice of pace car is a prestigious event for the American motor manufacturers as it guarantees massive publicity for the chosen model. The rest of the field are allowed to close up with care in single file behind the race leader.

As this vehicle has to set and maintain a reasonable speed the model chosen for the pace car is carefully chosen for its performance and wherever necessary is specially modified. In addition to modifications made for safety and speed, flashing lights are also added.

During this caution period drivers can only pass the pace car if its flashing lights are turned off, the on-board CART officials hand signal from the right-hand side is ceased, are signalled to do so by the same official, or a driver has entered the pit lane but not passed the 'blend line' of the pit exit. No driver may pass another car unless it is stopped on the track, or is on the inside of the track, or is not maintaining lap speed at the same pace, or both cars are in the pit lane.

As soon as possible after the yellow flags are displayed the pace car will take up position immediately in front of the leading car on the track, whether it is the actual race leader or not. If that car pulls off into the pit lane the pace car will position itself ahead of the next car leading on the track. If however, a car that was leading on the track or in the pit lane at the start of a full course yellow, or another car that could assume the lead as a result of a pit stop, returns onto the track ahead of a car that does not enter the pits, the pace car may move ahead of this car (got the idea?). All laps completed under a yellow caution flag are counted as official scoring laps and are counted toward completion of the race distance. If it at all possible the drivers will be warned before the pace car actually leaves the track. The signal to re-start is given when

Above
The scoring pylon at the Indianapolis Motor Speedway displays the position of each car in the race. (Duane J Appleget)

Right
*Emerson Fittipaldi pits during the Toyota
Monterey Grand Prix at Leguna Seca,
California, on 18 October 1992. The
Brazilian driver started in third place but
was plagued by mechanical problems
throughout the race and finished 19th.
(Marlboro)*

the pace car turns off its lights and accelerates away to its reserved area.

   The penalty for any driver passing another incorrectly while under yellow caution flag direction is an automatic two lap deduction.

Finishing positions

A race is officially over as soon as the lead car is given the chequered flag as it crosses the finishing line having completed the scheduled number of laps to complete the distance. If a race is stopped by a red flag and the leading cars have completed more than half the race distance, finishing positions will be set from the leaders last official lap scored.

Results

The race result is only 'official' 30 minutes after the race has ended, providing there is no protest. Any protest must be registered and a $500 fee paid within this 30 minute period otherwise the race result is signed by the race steward and becomes final.

THE CIRCUITS

IndyCar racing usually takes place on 16 circuits with the events staged throughout the season, which runs from March until October. Highspot of the IndyCar calender is undoubtedly the Indianapolis 500, which is staged at the end of May. Arguably the greatest event in motorsport, this prestigious race attracts over 500,000 spectators and a world-wide TV audience of about 500 million.

The circuits used for IndyCar racing are varied, ranging from the Super Speedway oval tracks (most of which are in fact rectangular), to road race circuits and temporary road courses.

The high speed oval tracks are the most demanding for the drivers as they require intense concentration for lap after lap with little room, if any, for error. The banked corners or turns also subject the drivers to tremendous physical forces during the race. Competitors must be in peak physical and mental condition to cope with the unrelenting pressures. Each turn on an oval track requires a very precise line if the driver is to maintain the optimum speed. There is no time relax; drivers are constantly aware that a lapse in concentration or mechanical failure can quickly result in an impact with the concrete outer wall, which is no joke when travelling at well over 200 mph. The difference between a quick, controlled exit through a turn and a collision with the wall is often a matter of mere inches.

The road race courses are the same as European purpose-built circuits and vary widely in there layout and location. For drivers these are the safer of the three venues due to the fact that they have run-off areas and are not lined by unforgiving concrete.

The other courses are temporary tracks set up on closed sections of public roads. These tend to attract the largest numbers of spectators for the simple reason that the locals have little, if any, distance to travel, and are sometimes able to watch races from their homes or gardens. Apart from the immediate economic benefits, cities like Long Beach in California are proud of their association with IndyCar racing.

The other race courses are just as tough but are generally more forgiving than the oval circuits. Road and street courses tend to have run-off areas and the longer straights allow drivers to 'relax'; more turns and the odd chicane provide a welcome respite from the hypnotic ovals. The variety of the circuits, and the different driving techniques needed to master them, is seen as a true test of racing ability

Above
A thoughtful Nigel Mansell seconds before venturing out onto an oval race circuit for the first time. (Dan R Boyd)

Above

Well Nigel, this is the gear lever! Mario Andretti introduces Nigel to the IndyCar he raced and helped develop, with his son Michael, during the 1992 season. Mansell had to re-aquaint himself with using a manual gearbox after a year of driving a semi-automatic Williams, in which the finger-operated gear selector is fitted underneath the steering wheel (Dan R Boyd)

1993 PPG INDYCAR WORLD SERIES VENUES

March 21 ROAD
AUSTRALIAN INDYCAR GP
SURFERS PARADISE, QUEENSLAND,
AUSTRALIA.

April 4 OVAL
VALVOLINE 200,
PHOENIX, ARIZONA

April 18 ROAD
TOYOTA GP
LONG BEACH, CALIFORNIA.

May 30 OVAL
INDIANAPOLIS 500,
INDIANAPOLIS ILLINOIS

June 6 OVAL
MILLER GENUINE DRAFT 200
MILWAUKEE

June 13 ROAD
ITT AUTOMOTIVE DETROIT GP
DETROIT

June 27 ROAD
BUDWEISER/GI JOE'S 200
PORTLAND

July 11 ROAD
CLEVELAND GP
CLEVELAND,OHIO

July 18 ROAD
MOLSON INDY TORONTO
TORONTO, CANADA

Aug 1 OVAL
MARLBORO 500
BROOKLYN, MI

Aug 8 OVAL
NEW ENGLAND 200
LONDON, NEW HAMPSHIRE

Aug 22 ROAD
TEXACO/HAVOLINE 200,
ELKHART LAKE, WI

Aug 29 ROAD
MOLSON INDY VANCOUVER
VANCOUVER, BC, CANADA

Sept 12 ROAD
PIONEER ELECTRONICS 200
LEXINGTON, OHIO

Sept 19 OVAL
BOSCH SPARK PLUG GP
NAZARETH, PA

Oct 3 ROAD
TOYOTA MONTEREY GP
MONTEREY, CALIFORNIA.

Frenzied Pennzoil pit action; only six crew can work on the car, the team member on the right steadying the tyre had better stay behind that wall.

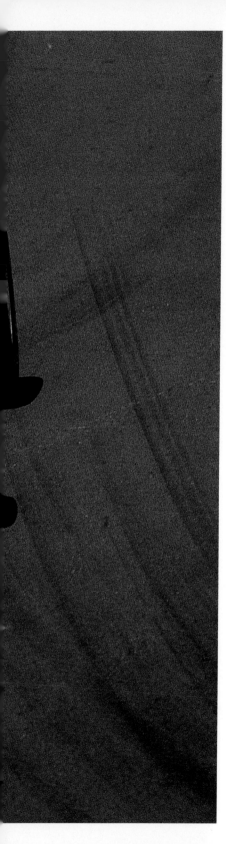

SURFERS PARADISE, QUEENSLAND AUSTRALIA
Opening venue for the IndyCar series is at the closed 2.793 mile road circuit, which has a demanding five straight sections linked by chicanes to give 16 turns. Surfers Paradise is popular with drivers because it closely resembles a race track in layout.

PHOENIX INTERNATIONAL RACEWAY
The one mile oval Phoenix International Raceway is located in the desert outside Phoenix, Arizona and features 11° banking in Turns One and Two and 9° in Turns Three and Four. According to the drivers conditions on the oval can change from lap to lap but the biggest problem is air turbulence from other cars. *(Pictures pp 54-57)*

LONG BEACH CALIFORNIA
The Long Beach circuit is close to Los Angeles and features two long straights joined by a series of turns at each end. The surface of the track is not ideal and makes passing difficult off the racing line. *(Pages 58-61)*

INDIANAPOLIS
The Indianapolis Motor Speedway is the most famous race track in the world; the circuit is 2.5 miles long with four turns and banked at 9°. The curbing added to each of the turns during the winter of 1992/93 has reduced the width of the track. *(Pages 60-68)*

WISCONSIN STATE FAIR PARK MILWAUKEE
Third of the oval venues, this is a one mile circuit with 9° of banking in all four turns. Relatively wide but extremely bumpy, Wisconsin is slower than comparable tracks and hard on tyres. *(Page 68)*

Left

Al Unser Jr in action in his Valvoline G92 Chevrolet at Surfers Paradise, Australia, on 22 March 1992. He started this, the first race in the '92 season, in pole position but in the closing laps on a wet circuit he was relegated to fourth place; team mate Danny Sullivan finished fifth. (Dan R Boyd/Galmer)

DETROIT MICHIGAN

The Detroit GP is staged at the Belle Isle Park circuit which is located on Belle Isle island in the middle of the Detroit river. It is a popular track despite being narrow and difficult to overtake on. *(Page 69)*

PORTLAND INTERNATIONAL RACEWAY

This purpose-built nine turn road circuit, located in Portland, Oregon, demands careful monitoring of fuel consumption because drivers accelerate hard down its two long straights. Portland has three 180° turns linking the two straights and these often create problems with back markers so races can be very close indeed.

CLEVELAND OHIO BURKE LAKEFRONT AIRPORT

This 2.37 mile, ten turn temporary road circuit utilises two runways and a taxiway at Burke Lakefront Airport, which is located next to Lake Erie in Cleveland, Ohio. It is the fastest road course in the IndyCar race schedule with 140 mph lap speed averages. As one would expect there is plenty of room to run off, which makes the track very safe, but drivers need to concentrate to overcome the lack of visual references that would normally help them to judge the turns. *(Page 72)*

TORONTO ONTARIO

The city streets of Canada's financial capital are the stage for the 1.78 mile Molson brewery race around the parkland of the Canadian National Exhibition Grounds next to Lake Ontario. It is a fast, smooth circuit and wide enough to allow plenty of places to pass. *(Page 70)*

MICHIGAN INTERNATIONAL SPEEDWAY

This two mile Super Speedway oval, one of three such circuits owned by Roger Penske, is located near Brooklyn 18 miles southeast of Jackson. It is extremely fast thanks to its 18° banked turns; the back straight is banked 5° and the front 12°. After buying the oval, Penske resurfaced the track to make it one of the fastest and toughest in the series. Its tough because of the high banking (18° in each of the four turns), and there's only one real straight. Because the course is so short more laps are covered than in the Indianapolis 500. *(Pages 74-81)*

Above

A pensive Al Unser Jr consults his pit crew before the start of the Valvoline 200 race at Phoenix International Raceway where he came home in fifth place. (Dan R Boyd/Galmer)

Above

*Final preparations in the Arizona
sunshine before the start of the
Valvoline 200 mile race at the one-mile
oval Phoenix International Raceway.
(Dan R Boyd/Galmer)*

NEW HAMPSHIRE INTERNATIONAL SPEEDWAY

This new one mile oval has a superb surface but the 12° banked turns
are tight, which makes the circuit very tough. While not as fast as the
Phoenix oval, it enables higher speeds than Milwaukee.

ROAD AMERICA ELK HART LAKE, WISCONSIN

This four mile circuit was constructed in the mid 1950s to provide a
motor racing venue close to the city of Chicago and the Canadian
border. One of the longest, fastest circuits in the United States, it is also
one of the most picturesque and demanding. With its fast straights and
tight turns, fuel consumption is again an important factor at Road
America; the pits are located at the top of a hill, so if a car runs out of
gas the driver at eliminated. *(Page 78-80)*

MOLSON INDY VANCOUVER BRITISH COLUMBIA, CANADA

The Molson Indy race is held on a nine turn, temporary road course around the British Columbia Place stadium in downtown Pacific Place, Vancouver, Canada. It is a popular event with Canadian racing fans but not with the drivers, as it is a very narrow course with few passing places.

MID-OHIO SPORTS CAR COURSE LEXINGTON, OHIO

First opened in 1962, it was not until the mid eighties, after being refurbished by the Trueman family, that this circuit began to emerge as one of America's major racing venues. The circuit is a challenging one: it is narrow, and combines a number of twists and turns with climbs and drops in height.

PENNSYLVANIA INTERNATIONAL RACEWAY

Nazareth, Pennsylvania is not just famous for being the home of the legendary Andretti family – it also has an oval track that was formerly the semi-banked dirt 1.4 mile D-shaped oval built in 1966. The new one mile tri-oval, located 50 miles from Philadelphia and 80 miles from New York City, has Turn One banked 3°, Turn Two 4° and Turn Three 6°. The Pennsylvania Raceway is unique in having a 0.75 mile warm up lane separate from the racing surface. This feature allows slower moving cars to warm up their engines and tyres without hampering faster competitors. Narrow and with no margin for error, this is a very demanding oval.

LAGUNA SECA RACEWAY MONTEREY, CALIFORNIA

Built on a similar pattern to the Mid-Ohio course, the hugely demanding 2.2 mile Leguna Seca circuit is located in the foothills of California's Monterey Peninsula. Amazingly, the circuit attracts huge crowds despite being 100 miles south of San Francisco. Built in 1956 in collaboration with the US Army, the Raceway replaced the former Pebble Beach course, which was based on public roads The track has a number of changes in elevation and at least four places where overtaking is easy. (Pages 82-85)

Left

Warming up the tyres before the start of the Valvoline 200 at Phoenix International Raceway on 5 April 1992, which was won by Bobby Rahal in the Miller Genuine Draft 192 Chevy V8/A. He dominated the race from start to finish and scored his first victory as owner/driver. (David Taylor/Colorsport)

Above

Nigel Mansell leads the opening laps of the round three PPG IndyCar World Series Toyota Grand Prix at Long Beach, California, 1993. Paul Tracy caught him on lap 4 from which point the Canadian went on to win. (Duane J Appleget)

Right

John Andretti in the Pennzoil Special during practice for the Toyota GP at Long Beach, on 12 April 1992 where he finished 20th. (Michael Dunn/Pennzoil)

Above

John Andretti in his Hall/VDS Racing Pennzoil Special 1992 Lola-Chevy at the Indy 500 where number 8 finished eighth. (Michael Dunn/Pennzoil)

Right

Long Beach, 18 April 1993. The race was marked by an unusally large number of crashes. One of the victims was Al Unser Jr who collided with Mansell exiting Turn Two. Mansell survived to take third place, despite losing second gear with 30 laps to go. (Michael Dunn/Pennzoil)

Above
The 1992 Indy 500 winner, Al Unser Jr poses with car constructor Alan Mertens and team owner Rick Galles for the post-race photos. The car is lined up along the famous 'yard of bricks', visible in the foreground. The Borg-Warner trophy, on the left, will soon acquire a profile effigy of the winner. The trophy stands over four feet high, weighs 80 lbs and is made of sterling silver. It features the bas-relief bust of every Indianapolis 500 winner since 1911. (Dan R Boyd/Galmer)

Above right
Conpare the same Galmer car in the same year, but set up in road course trim, with those large front wings. (Dan R Boyd/Galmer)

Right
There are several clues to the fact that this is qualifying, Indy 500, 1993, and not race day. The easiest is the empty stand. The 500 is the biggest paying spectator sports event in the world. (Duane J Appleget)

Above

Scotsman Jim Crawford, in the Quaker State King 192 Buick, spins in Turn Two and is about to collect Rick Mears as John Andretti takes avoiding action. (Duane J Appleget)

Left

To the victor the spoils: a customary pint of milk for Al Unser Jr in victory lane. He had just won the 76th Indy 500 by 0.043 sec from Scott Goodyear, the closest margin in IndyCar history. (Michael Dunn/Pennzoil)

Above
Philippe Gache in his Formula Project Rhone Poulenc Rorer car, a '91 Lola Chevrolet
Indy V8/A entered by Dick Simon Racing, waves his arm to show that he is okay after
being shunted into the wall at over 120 mph by Stan Fox. (Duane J Appleget)

Above right
Danny Sullivan crashed in Turn One. Here the right-hand side of the car disintegrates,
absorbing the crash energy. (Duane J Appleget)

Right
The destruction continues ... note the nose cone flying up and over the drivers head.
When the car finally stopped Danny Sullivan was uninjured thanks to the strength of
the tub. (Duane J Appleget)

Above
Turn Four in the Miller Genuine Draft 200 race at the historic Milwaukee Mile track in Wisconsin. John Andretti, who finished ninth, shadows the Galmer of Danny Sullivan, who crossed the line in seventh place.(Michael Dunn/Pennzoil)

Right
John Andretti qualifying for the Detroit GP in June 1992. He was forced to retire with gearbox trouble after 26 laps. The race was won by Bobby Rahal in his Miller Genuine Draught L92 Chevy V8/A. (Michael Dunn/Pennzoil)

Close company! Emerson Fittipaldi leads his new team mate Paul Tracy during practice for the Molson Indy Toronto in Canada. Both would be forced to retire in 1992. But Tracy won the 1993 event in a Marlboro Chevy Penske V8/C in front of his home crowd; and second place gave 50-year-old Fittipaldi a narrow lead in the PPG World Series. (Marlboro)

Mario Andretti driving the 1992 Lola Ford Cosworth XB. In 1989 Mario and Michael became the first father-son team in IndyCar. In the last race of the 1992 season, the Toyota Monterey GP, they took first and second, separated at the finish by just 4.715 seconds. (Dan R Boyd/Newman-Haas)

Left

Jim Hall, co-owner of the Hall/VDS Racing Pennzoil Lola Chevrolet, consults with his driver John Andretti before the start of the Michigan 500 race; Andretti finished a lap down in sixth place. (Linda Dunn/Pennzoil)

Above

John Andretti passes Tony Bettenhausen in the Amax Energy + Metals PC20 Penske 1991 Chevy V8/A during the Michigan 500. Another example of keeping it in the family: Tony's father competed in 14 Indy 500s. (Michael Dunn/Pennzoil)

Overleaf

Pit stop action for John Andretti in the same race. Although he only managed to qualify in 14th place, John finished 6th. (Michael Dunn/Pennzoil)

Above

No room for error! Rick Mears in action with the Marlboro Penske Chevrolet. Here at Milwaukee for the Miller Genuine Draught 200, June 2, 1991. From pole position he was forced out of the running after 140 laps with ignition failure. (Marlboro)

Left

Turn Five, lap one in the Texaco Havoline 200 race at the Road America circuit at Elkhart Lake, Wisconsin. Mario Andretti leads nephew John Andretti, who is in front of Danny Sullivan who in turn is followed by Michael Andretti. (Michael Dunn/Pennzoil)

Above

Despite driving hard throughout the race Al Unser Jr finished in fourth place at Michigan. He had started the race way down the grid in 15th place. The 12 points he gained put him into 2nd place in the championship. (Dan R Boyd/Galmer)

Left

A brief pit stop for John Andretti watched closely by a CART observer. The boom extending out from the pit wall has a welcome drink for the driver on the end of it. (Linda Dunn/Pennzoil)

Above

Paul Tracy in race number 4, the Marlboro Penske Chevrolet V8/B, leads fellow Canadian Scott Goodyear in race number 15, the Mackenzie Financial 192 Chevrolet V8/A. (Marlboro)

Left

John Andretti leads Scott Pruett in the Budweiser Eagle 'Made in America' Truesports TR92C Chevrolet V8/A powered car at the Toyota Monterey Grand Prix at Leguna Seca, California. (Pennzoil)

Overleaf

Paul Tracy moves out onto the track during practice for the Toyota Monterey GP. In the race Tracy started second and chased Michael Andretti for the lead until, with just four laps to go and a second down on the leader, he and Jimmy Vasser collided in Turn 11. (Marlboro)

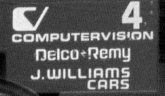

Teams and personalities

Inevitably, like most motor sports, IndyCar racing is an expensive business. Most race teams require a budget approaching £1 million to over £4 million each season. The budget includes drivers' salaries, the wages of all the team personnel, their travel and accommodation expenses, and the cost of buying or building a 'rolling chassis' – a basic car but without an engine. Each team will aim to ideally have three cars per driver: one as the main race car, the second as a fully prepared race spare and the third as a development machine.

In the search for winning power teams will often use more than ten engines in a season. These cost in the region of £30,000 to £70,000 each and need to be rebuilt after each track session. At a typical IndyCar race weekend, a car will need at least seven engines: two for practice and the race, with another two as back ups in case there are any problems. Two engines are usually being rebuilt while the other rebuilt engine is in transit. Apart from a different fuel injection system set up, the engines are all the same for each of the different types of track. The fine tuning of the engine is largely controlled by highly sophisticated fuel management systems.

The engines, chassis and salaries account for a large slice of the race budget, added to which is the cost of spare parts, wheels, tyres, a transporter vehicle and of course the price of around 400,000 US gallons of methanol.

Obviously winning doesn't come cheap, so teams depend upon sponsors for capital. The range of sponsors, excluding the usual automotive connected companies, is continually expanding as the sport grows in popularity. IndyCar attracts massive world-wide interest through television, ensuring that each sponsor gains valuable, high profile publicity and marketing potential in return for its investment. Cars become high speed advertisements with the driver, team personnel and their transport promoting the image, so it's not surprising that companies are prepared to commit large sums to fund the winning formula.

TEAM NEWMAN-HAAS RACING

One of the most well-known IndyCar race teams is that of Carl Haas and famous actor Paul Newman. Although not as well known outside of the sport as the team's co-owner, Carl Haas's wealth of experience makes him the managing partner. Their association began in 1983 when

Above
Lynn St James, who began her IndyCar racing career in 1992, was only the second woman to start the Indy 500. St James worked her way up from 27th place to finish 11th – a fine achievement for a rookie. (Duane J Appleget)

Paul Newman signed up as co-partner with businessman Carl Haas, who was then the North American importer for Lola Cars Ltd. For Newman his interest in the sport was spurred in 1968 while he was working on the motion picture *Winning*, in which he played the role of a driver in the Indianapolis 500. Newman began his racing career in 1972 and over the years he has proved himself highly competitive by winning four Sports Car Club of America national amateur championships. Before joining Carl Haas in IndyCar, Paul Newman was involved with the Can-Am series, where his drivers included Al Unser, Danny Sullivan, Teo Fabi, Keke Rosberg and Bobby Rahal.

The partners first signed up Mario Andretti; then in 1989 they made history by signing up his son Michael, thereby creating the first father and son racing team in the IndyCar series. Their faith in Andretti talent was rewarded when Michael won two races in 1989, five during 1990 and the 1991 PPG IndyCar World Series Championship. This was achieved by winning a record eight races and eight pole positions. Commenting on Michael's achievement, Carl Haas opined: 'I think he's the fastest driver on this circuit. He'd have no problem with Formula One. I think Mike would quickly become a star in Formula One'.

Michael Andretti's talents were further demonstrated during the 1992 season in June with wins at Portland and Road America. It was therefore not surprising that Michael announced his intention of driving in Formula One the following season. Unfortunately, his start in Formula

Above
Carl Haas, with the ever present (but rarely lit) Havana cigar. (Dan R Boyd/Newman-Haas)

Right
The 1992 Newman-Haas line-up comprised (left to right) Carl Haas, Michael Andretti, Mario Andretti and Paul Newman. The team had been the PPG IndyCar World Series Champions the previous year, Michael Andretti being the winning driver. (Newman-Haas)

One was inauspicious; DNF became the norm for him at the beginning of the 1993 season.

To replace him the partner's seized upon the opportunity offered up by Nigel Mansell's decision, made in September at Monza, to leave F1 and signed up the new World Champion to partner Mario Andretti during 1993 in the Kmart/Havoline Lola Ford Cosworth. The two drivers were former team mates briefly in 1980 for the Lola Grand Prix team and looked forward to renewing their partnership.

Newman-Haas' major sponsors are Kmart, Texaco Havoline Racing, Bosch, Corning, BASF, Energizer, Dirt Devil, Gillette and Alexander Julian Menswear, giving the team a solid financial base for success.

Above
Race overalls are invariably festooned with advertising and sponsorship logos. Wonder if Nigel Mansell's deal with upmarket London department store Harrods includes a free Christmas hamper? (Newman/Haas)

Right
New world champion, new year and a new type of race car. Thirty-nine-year-old Nigel Mansell tries an IndyCar cockpit for the first time. (Dan R Boyd)

MARIO ANDRETTI

The old man of the Andretti clan is out in front of everyone in IndyCar; by the end of the '92 season he had chalked up an amazing 376 starts and looks set to pass the 400 mark in '93.

He began IndyCar racing in 1964 at Trenton, New Jersey, where he finished eleventh. Over the following years he scored an impressive 51 IndyCar wins beginning with the 1965 Hoosier GP, while his last victory to-date occurred at the 1993 Cleveland, Phoenix 200. Andretti's score sheet also includes 64 pole positions and he looks forward to more success with the Kmart/Havoline Lola Ford Cosworth: 'Winning is what it's all about'.

His son Michael followed him into IndyCar in 1983 and up until this year, when he announced his intention to enter Formula One, was a leading contender in the series. He scored his first victory at Long Beach

Above

Mario Andretti waits patiently for the start in his Lola Ford. Inside the helmet he can hear the final countdown on his two-way radio ... (Duane J Appleget)

Above

Life in the fast lane: more than a decade after leaving the Lola GP team, Mario Andretti and Nigel Mansell are back together again at Newman-Haas. They are also both ex-Team Lotus campaigners. (Dan R Boyd)

in 1986 and had racked up 27 by the end of the '92 season. The year before was his most successful when he took eight of the races, setting a new CART record and taking the PPG championship title.

Nineteen ninety-one was a great year for the Andretti family: at the Milwaukee 200 Michael Andretti finished first, John Andretti, (Mario Andretti's nephew) was second, Mario Andretti was third and Jeff Andretti, his youngest son, was 11th – a real family affair!

*Nineteen-ninety-two IndyCar Champion
Bobby Rahal compares notes with 1992
Formula One World Champion, Nigel
Mansell. Until turbo wastgate problems
forced him to retire on lap 56 of the
Molsen Indy at Toronto on July 18,
Mansell had maintained an unbroken
lead in the 1993 Series. Emerson
Fittipaldi's fine 2nd behind hard-charging
Chevy Penske team mate Paul Tracy – a
repeat of their emphatic performance at
Cleveland a week earlier – put him two
points clear of Mansell and fellow-
Brazilan Raul Boesel. (Dan R Boyd)*

Above
Alan Mertens, the British engineer whose Galmer Engineering company, based in Bicester, Oxford, produced Al Unser Jr's 1992 Indy winning car. (Galmer)

Left
Rick Galles, owner of Galles Racing International, whose team won the 1990 PPG World Series and the 1992 Indianapolis 500 with driver Al Unser Jr. (Galles Racing)

GALLES RACING INTERNATIONAL

Formerly the Galles Racing Team, started by Rick Galles and Maury Kraines in 1990 as a joint project, this partnership dissolved at the end of the 1992 season. Back in November 1988, a research and development facility was established in the UK with English mechanical engineer Alan Mertens. Galmer (GALles-MERtens) began by developing the Lola chassis, but in August 1991 they had designed their own G91 chassis using the expertise and components of associated British companies, such as Ilmor, Advanced Composites, Pi, Dymag, and Alcon.

Driver Al Unser Jnr, son of famous IndyCar driver Al Unser and nephew to Bobby Unser, won the 1990 championship for the Galles-Kraco team. In 1992, using an updated G92 chassis, Al Unser Jr and team mate Danny Sullivan led the opening race at Surfers Paradise until rain slowed them down. A couple of weeks later in the Toyota Grand Prix round at Long Beach in California, Al Jr was leading Danny Sullivan but a misunderstanding between them on the last lap gave the victory to Sullivan. A month later at the Indianapolis 500, a determined Al Unser Jr fought a tough race to narrowly snatch the crowning glory for the team. In a close fought season, Al Unser Jr, who had invested his own money in the car's Galmer chassis, went on to finish third in the championship with Danny Sullivan seventh. For 1993 the team reverted to a Lola chassis with sponsorship from Valvoline and Molson.

AL UNSER JR

Al Unser Jr ('Little Al'), is the son of four-times Indianapolis winner Al Unser and the nephew of three-times winner Bobby Unser and the late Jerry Unser who was killed in the Indy 500 in 1958.

He began his IndyCar career in 1982 when he was 20-years-old at the Riverside International Raceway in California, starting in tenth place he finished fifth, having passed A J Foyt, Gordon Johncock and his father. As Al recalls, 'Next to my dad and uncle Bobby, the drivers I most admired while growing up were A J Foyt and Gordon Johncock and when I passed them and my dad it was like I lost something and at the same time became one of them'. His first IndyCar victory came a little later on Fathers Day 1984 at the Portland International Raceway. In 1985 he joined the Doug Shierson Team with whom he won consecutive races at New Jersey Meadowlands and Cleveland and ended the season second in the championship; he lost out to his father by just one point, 150 to 151.

In 1989 Al Unser Jr achieved his first pole position at Long Beach California and won the race, but at Indianapolis he was just beaten into second place by Emerson Fittipaldi. On his way to his first IndyCar championship in 1990, Al won six races, his four consecutive victories at

Above
*Al Unser Jr poses with his Galmer 92
IndyCar. (Dan R Boyd/Galmer)*

Toronto, Michigan International Speedway, Denver and Vancouver being a new IndyCar record. The victory at Michigan was his first 500 miler and was also the fastest 500 mile race ever run, with an average speed of 189.727 mph. In 1991 'Little Al' had thirteen top five finishes and ended the season third in the championship. He chalked up another record in 1992 by finishing 23 races in a row. To date he has won 18 races and will no doubt score many more successes in IndyCar.

DANNY SULLIVAN

Danny Sullivan was once a New York City cab driver but worked his way up through Formula Ford, Can-Am and Formula 3 before starting IndyCar racing in 1982 at Atlanta where he finished third, setting an unbroken record for a rookie driver. At Indianapolis that year he qualified 13th but finished 14th after hitting the wall. In 1983 he drove in

Above
Danny Sullivan at Nazareth; from cab driver to the fastest 500 mile race ever run, at Michigan. (Colorsport)

Right
Al Unser Jr. In 1985, Junior lost out to his father in the Championship by just one point. Racing dynasties are one of the most remarkable aspects of IndyCar. (Dan R Boyd/Galmer)

Formula One, scoring a fifth at Monaco. Sullivan returned to IndyCars in 1984, winning at Cleveland, Pocono, Montreal and achieving nine, top-ten finishes to come fourth in the championship. The following year he won the Indianapolis 500 despite spinning in front of Mario Andretti on lap 120. In 1988 he won his first PPG championship with the Penske Team and scored his last win for them at Leguna Seca in 1990. He then joined Patrick Racing in 1991 to race the Alfa-Romeo before moving to Galles in 1992, for whom he won the Long Beach race in the Galmer car. Sullivan drove the new Lola in '93.

Above
AJ Foyt at Laguna Seca, 1985. In 1993, after symbolically parking his car on the start/finish line at the Indianapolis Motor Speedway, 'AJ' was moved to tears (as were many of his devoted fans) when he announced his snap decision to retire to the crowds on official qualifying day. (Colorsport)

Above

AJ Foyt being interviewed by IMS radio network. Foyt's decision to hang up his helmet at Indianapolis was apparently influenced by the sight of Robby Gordon crashing at the start of the official qualifying session. (Duane J Appleget)

A J FOYT JR

The legendary Anthony Joseph Foyt Jr began racing IndyCars in 1957 and was the first driver to win the Indianapolis 500 four times (1961,1964,1967 and 1977). In a racing career spanning over 35 years he has won 67 races and 53 pole positions. In 1964 he scored an incredible ten victories (of which seven were consecutive) from 13 starts, a record only equalled by Al Unser in 1970. A crash in 1990 resulted in serious leg injuries but the tough Texan battled back to fitness in time for the following season – to the great delight of millions of race fans. In recognition of his accomplishments in the IndyCar series, CART officially retired his famous number 14.

Above

Formula One World Champion in 1972 and 1974, the popular Brazilian driver Emerson Fittipaldi began IndyCar racing in 1984 and has won 17 races, including the Indianapolis 500 in 1989. Fittipaldi enjoyed a successful season in 1992, winning at Surfers Paradise, Cleveland, Elkhart Lake and Mid-Ohio (Dan R Boyd/Marlboro)

Left

Rick Mears announced his retirement in December 1992. He was IndyCar Champion three times (1979, 1981 and 1982), and won the Indianapolis 500 four times (1979, 1984, 1988 and 1991). In addition, Mears remains the only driver to win six Indianapolis 500 poles and the only driver to win every road race in a single season, a feat he achieved in 1981. (Dan R Boyd/Marlboro)

RICK MEARS

'Rocket Rick' Mears, sometimes called the 'Ovalmeister', is another of the three racing legends to have achieved four wins at Indianapolis; for his 20 wins in the 1980s he was named Driver of the Decade by the Associated Press in 1990. Mears is also ranked in the top six in lifetime victories, pole positions, laps led and is the all-time leader in earnings. He began his IndyCar career in 1976 at the California 500 where he finished eighth, earning the title USAC Rookie of the Year. Late in 1977 he was hired by Roger Penske to replace Mario Andretti, who had left the team to pursue the F1 world championship. In his debut at Indianapolis, Mears amazed the established stars by making the front row of the grid and went on to win races at Milwaukee, Atlanta and Brands Hatch. Mears looked set to go for his fifth Indy win in '93, but announced his surprise retirement at Penske Racing's end of season party.

EMERSON FITTIPALDI

Emerson, the son of the famous racing journalist Wilson Fittipaldi, began racing in Brazil but moved to the UK to race in Formula Ford. In 1969 he won eight of 11 Formula 3000 races and came to the attention of Colin Chapman at Lotus, who offered him a Formula One drive for 1970. With Team Lotus he won his first F1 race on 4 October 1970 at Watkins Glen. By 1972 he had won his first F1 World Championship at the age of 25. In 1974 he scored his second F1 title success with Marlboro McLaren. In 1976 Fittipaldi formed his own F1 team with his brother, Wilson Jr. Due to financial difficulties the team was destined to fail and in 1982 Fittipaldi retired from F1 to pursue his business interests back in Brazil. But by 1984 he was racing again, this time in IndyCar, making his debut at Long Beach, California. The following season, on 28 July 1985, he won his first race: the Marlboro 500 for the 7-Eleven/Patrick Team. His other victories include the Indianapolis 500 in 1989 with the Marlboro/Patrick team. A driver with the Penske Team since 1990, Fittipaldi has 17 race wins and 13 pole positions to his credit at the time of writing.

BOBBY RAHAL

The winner of the 1992 IndyCar Championship began racing in 1982 and won his first race at the Cleveland 500. Rahal took his second win at the Michigan 150 and finished the season in an outstanding second place. In 1986 Rahal achieved his ambition and won his first Indianapolis 500 and went on to win the CART National Championship by beating Mario Andretti; a year later Rahal repeated the feat and once again Andretti had to settle for second place in series. Since then Rahal has been consistently near the top in IndyCar racing. In 1991 he formed his own team, Rahal-Hogan Racing, with partner Carl Hogan and promptly won four races and the PPG Championship. Rahal will be keen to retain his title in 1993.

ARIE LUYENDYK

Arie Luyendyk began his racing career in Formula One before turning his attention to IndyCars in 1984, coming eighth in his debut at Elkhart Lake. In 1985 he qualified 20th at Indianapolis and finished the race in a creditable seventh place. Fortune did not smile on him for the next few years, but in 1990 his efforts were rewarded when he qualified on the front row of the grid at Indy and went on to win the race. The following year he drove for Vince Granatelli Racing, scoring wins at Phoenix and Nazareth, but during 1992 was unable to compete due to lack of finance. Luyendyk returned full-time in 1993 with the Chip Ganassi Team.

WILLIAM STOKKAN

Bill Stokkan is chairman as well as chief executive officer of CART and has been largely responsible for streamlining the organisation into a total sports entertainment enterprise. He developed his business skills by promoting *Playboy* magazine, a success story that he also envisages for IndyCar.

Right
Bobby Rahal, runner-up in the 1991 season, in action in his STP-Kraco 191 Chevrolet, race number 18. He started the Valvoline 200 race at Phoenix in 4th place and had to have his 2nd place finish confirmed by video. (STP/Kraco)

ROGER PENSKE

The co-founder of the CART organisation has been involved with motorsports for over 30 years, most of it with IndyCar as a team leader. Back in 1978, determined to get the owners more involved in the rule making and administration of the sport, Penske joined forces with U E 'Pat' Patrick to form Championship Auto Racing Teams Inc. This gave teams, drivers and sponsors an equal voice in discussions with the USAC board of control. Penske Racing has been one of the most successful teams ever in IndyCar and utilises research and development facilities at Poole in Dorset, England.

AL UNSER

Another legend in IndyCar racing, Unser has also won the Indy 500 on four occasions as well as being one of only three drivers (with Mario Andretti and A J Foyt Jr), to win races on road tracks, paved ovals and dirt tracks in a single season. He began racing in 1964 and drove full-time until 1985. Since then Unser has been called upon by a number of teams to replace injured drivers, as in 1987 when he substituted for Danny Ongais at the request of Penske Racing and won the Indy 500. True to form, in 1992 he stepped in to replace the injured Nelson Piquet and finished in third place at the Speedway, the highest place ever for a Buick-powered car at the track.

NIGEL MANSELL

Newcomer to the IndyCar scene for the 1993 season is the Formula One World Champion Nigel Mansell, OBE.

Nigel Mansell began his F1 career in 1980 and since his first Grand Prix win on 6 October 1985, at Brands Hatch in the GP of Europe, has been in the top echelons of the sport.

He became the most successful English racing car driver in history at the Magny Cours circuit in July 1991 when he won the French Grand Prix – his 17th victory. This also proved to be the first of a hat-trick of wins, with victory following at the British GP at Silverstone and the German GP at Hockenheim. In 1992 Mansell made his presence felt by winning the first three races of the year; his second place in August at the Hungarian GP gave him the Championship. A contractural disagreement with Williams-Renault boss Frank Williams eventually resulted in the new champion signing for Newman-Haas Racing and IndyCar at the end of the F1 season. At the time of writing, speculation is rife as to Mansell's plans for 1994 and beyond. Bill Stokkan of CART has been making every effort to keep the Englishman working in the US.

Above
Arie Luyendyk drives for the Chip Ganassi Racing Team in the Target Scotch Video IndyCar. (Dan R Boyd/Chip Gannassi Racing)

Right
Roger Penske, is the owner of Penske Racing and co-founder of CART (Championship Auto Racing Teams, Inc). The team relies upon chassis designed and built at Penske's research and development centre at Poole in Dorset, England. (Penske Racing)

PAUL TRACY

Canadian Paul Tracy began his IndyCar career in 1991 with Dale Coyne Racing, but changed teams mid season to join Penske Racing as a test driver. He is considered to be among the most promising drivers in IndyCar and was named by *Automobile* magazine as one of 1992's Racing Stars of the Future.

SCOTT GOODYEAR

Fellow Canadian Scott Goodyear started racing at the age of nine in karts. In June 1987 he began his first season in IndyCar, finishing seventh in the Toronto Molson race. After only his third race at Indianapolis, starting 33rd (and last) on the grid for the famous 500 in 1992, Goodyear came second to Al Unser Jr by a mere 1/500th of a second – the closest and most spectacular finish ever seen at the Speedway.

Above
Arie Luyendyk in the groove during the Marlboro 500 at Michigan International Speedway on 2 August 1992; in only his second race of the season, Luyendyk was running well until a broken clutch relegated him to 14th place. (Dan R Boyd/Marlboro)

Right
Team owner Chip Ganassi utilises an R&D centre in West Sussex, England. (Dan R Boyd/Chip Ganassi Racing)

Above and left
Canadian Paul Tracy began his third IndyCar season in 1993. he won three races in succession (at Portland, Cleveland and Toronto). His victory at Cleveland earned newly married Tracy a $100,000 bonus. (Colorsport above, Walker Motorsports left)

Above
*Dehydration can be a big problem for
the drivers, especially in long races
during hot weather. Scott Goodyear
cools down with some well earned
refreshment. (Walker Motorsports)*

Goodyear went one better at the Michigan 500 in August that year and
made history by becoming the first Canadian to win an oval event.
Driving the Walker Motorsports, Mackenzie Financial Special Lola Ford,
he promises to be a major contender for the '93 crown.

JIM HALL

Former racer Jim Hall, co-owner of Hall-VDS Racing with engine builder
Franz Weiss, is widely recognised as the man who introduced 'ground
effects' to motor racing with the Pennzoil Chapparal car in 1979. During
1980 his driver, Johnny Rutherford, won the Indy 500 and four other
races; combined with other top finishes it gave Hall the first ever
combination of a CART PPG Cup IndyCar World Series Championship
and a United States Auto Club title. Disappointed with the increasingly
political nature of motor racing, Hall left IndyCar in 1982 to concentrate

on his other business interests. However, he returned in 1991 with another bright yellow Pennzoil sponsored car in the form of a Lola Chevrolet. His driver, John Andretti, won the first race of the season, the Australian Gold Coast Grand Prix, and further success brought the team to eighth place in the series, a performance repeated in 1992. For 1993 Jim Hall was looking for greater things with Teo Fabi in the Pennzoil Special. 'If everything goes right we can win. It will be hard, but we expect that.'

He was speaking for every driver, every sponsor, every team member, every fan of this magnificent motor sport.

Above
Canadian Scott Goodyear in the Mackenzie Financial Special Lola Chevy of Walker Motorsports (Walker Motorsports)

Right
Jim Hall, co-owner of the Hall/VDS team at Long Beach, California. (Michael Dunn/Pennzoil)

Facts and figures

CHAMPIONSHIP WINNERS 1909 TO 1992

YEAR	DRIVER	POINTS						
1909	George Robertson	1480 AAA	1946	Ted Horn	1360	1979	A J Foyt Jr	3320 USAC
1910	Ray Harroun	1240	1947	Ted Horn	1920	1979	Rick Mears	4060 CART
1911	Ralph Mulford	1545	1948	Ted Horn	1880	1980	Johnny Rutherford	4723 CART
1912	Ralph De Palma	2000	1949	Jonnie Parsons	2280			CRL
1913	Earl Cooper	2610	1950	Henry Banks	1390			
1914	Ralph De Palma	2045	1951	Tony Bettenhausen Sr	2556.6	1981	Rick Mears	304
1915	Earl Cooper	3780	1952	Chuck Stevenson	1440	1982	Rick Mears	294
1916	Dario Resta	4100	1953	Sam Hanks	1659.5	1983	Al Unser	151
1917	Earl Cooper	1095	1954	Jimmy Bryan	2630	1984	Mario Andretti	176
1918	Ralph Mulford	500	1955	Bob Swikert	2290 AAA	1985	Al Unser	151
1919	Howard Wilcox	1110	1956	Jim Bryan	1860 USAC	1986	Bobby Rahal	179
1920	Tommy Milton	2095	1957	Jimmy Bryan	1650	1987	Bobby Rahal	188
1921	Tommy Milton	2230	1958	Tony Bettenhausen Sr	1830	1988	Danny Sullivan	182
1922	Jimmy Murphy	3420	1959	Rodger Ward	2400	1989	Emerson Fittipaldi	196
1923	Eddie Hearne	1882	1960	A J Foyt Jr	1680	1990	Al Unser Jr	210
1924	Jimmy Murphy	1595	1961	A J Foyt Jr	2150	1991	Michael Andretti	234
1925	Peter De Paulo	3260	1962	Rodger Ward	2460	1992	Bobby Rahal	196
1926	Harry Hartz	2954	1963	A J Foyt Jr	2950			
1927	Peter De Paulo	1440	1964	A J Foyt Jr	2900			
1928	Louis Meyer	1596	1965	Mario Andretti	3110			
1929	Louis Meyer	1330	1966	Mario Andretti	3070			
1930	Billy Arnold	1027.5	1967	A J Foyt Jr	3440			
1931	Louis Schneider	712.5	1968	Bobby Unser	4330			
1932	Bob Carey	815	1969	Mario Andretti	5025			
1933	Louis Meyer	610	1970	Al Unser	5130			
1934	Bill Cummings	681.72	1971	Joe Leonard	3016			
1935	Kelly Petillo	890	1972	Joe Lenard	3460			
1936	Mauri Rose	1020	1973	Roger McCluskey	3705			
1937	Wilbur Shaw	1135	1974	Bobby Unser	4870			
1938	Floyd Roberts	1000	1975	A J Foyt Jr	4920			
1939	Wilbur Shaw	1000	1976	Gordon Johncock	4240			
1940	Rex Mays	1225	1977	Tom Sneva	3965			
1941	Rex Mays	1225	1978	Tom Sneva	4153			

Ted Horn is only driver to have won Indianapolis three times in succession (1946, 1947-48), and his hat-trick is unlikely to be repeated. Three drivers have won the Indy 500 four times: the great A J Foyt in 1961, 1964, 1967 and 1977; Al Unser Sr in 1970, 1971, 1978 and 1987; and Rick Mears in 1979, 1984, 1988 and 1991.

Above Right
Emerson Fittipaldi's Marlboro Penske '92 Chevy V8/B car fitted with speedway front spoilers

Right
The complexities of an IndyCar! (Dan R Boyd/Galmer)

NATIONAL CHAMPIONSHIP INDYCAR WINNERS ALL-TIME INDYCAR ROAD CIRCUIT POSITIONS

RACE WINNERS 1909-1992

Mario Andretti	21
Michael Andretti	19
Al Unser Jr	15
Bobby Rahal	14
Emerson Fittipaldi	13
Ralph De Palma	10
Earl Cooper	10
Danny Sullivan	9
Dan Gurney	7
Rick Mears	7
Bobby Unser	5
Al Unser	5

POLE POSITION WINNERS 1930-1992

Mario Andretti	26
Michael Andretti	26
Danny Sullivan	18
Bobby Rahal	13
Dan Gurney	10
Emerson Fittipaldi	10
Al Unser	8
Teo Fabi	5
Bobby Unser	5
Roberto Guerrero	4
Rick Mears	4
Al Unser Jr	3
Kevin Cogan	2
Danny Ongais	2
Lloyd Ruby	2

TOP 500 MILE DRIVERS, IN POLES, STARTS, WINS

500-MILE STARTS

A J Foyt Jr	69
Al Unser	63
Mario Andretti	62
Johnny Rutherford	59
Gordon Johncock	52
Tom Sneva	46
Pancho Carter	45
Rick Mears	41
Bobby Unser	40

500-MILE POLES

Rick Mears	15
A J Foyt Jr	10
Tom Sneva	7
Mario Andretti	6
Bobby Unser	5
Johnny Rutherford	4
Rex Mays	4
Emerson Fittipaldi	4

500-MILE WINS

A J Foyt Jr	9
Al Unser	8
Bobby Unser	8
Rick Mears	8
Johnny Rutherford	5
Danny Sullivan	4
Mario Andretti	3
Gordon Johncock	3
Louis Meyer	3
Wilber Shaw	3

Right
Nigel Mansell and Mario Andretti wear overalls made by Sparco, the French racewear manufacturers. The suits are double layer Nomex, although a triple layer is used on the back and the chest. The white colour of the design reduces the flame resistance due to the dye so an extra layer is added. (Dan R Boyd)

WINNING INDYCAR ENGINE MAKES

Number of wins	Make	Time span
99	OFFENHAUSER	1947-55
98	OFFENHAUSER	1955-63
81	COSWORTH	1981-86
37	CHEVROLET	1989-92

WINNING INDYCAR CHASSIS CONSTRUCTORS

Number of wins	Make	Time span
29	MILLER	1927-30
21	MILLER	1926-27
18	MILLER	1922-24
15	MILLER	1931-34
13	MARCH	1985-86
10	Pc-7	1979
8	WATSON	1963-64
8	LOLA	1984
7	KURTIS	1952-53
7	LOLA	1990
7	PEUGEOT	1916
1	PENSKE	1991
1	GALMER	1992

FASTEST INDYCAR RACE TRACKS

FASTEST OVAL

NAZARETH
PENNSYLVANIA INTERNATIONAL RACEWAY
181.435 MPH

FASTEST SUPER SPEEDWAY

INDIANAPOLIS MOTOR SPEEDWAY
232.618 MPH

FASTEST ROAD COURSE

ROAD AMERICA ELKHART LAKE
134.446 MPH

FASTEST TEMPORARY ROAD COURSE

CLEVELAND BURKE LAKEFRONT AIRPORT
142.778 MPH

FASTEST STREET COURSE

TORONTO ONTARIO CANADA
108.050 MPH

Right
The Chevrolet V8/A engine of Al Unser Jr. The engine is built in Britain by ILmor Engineering, once it reaches the other side of the Atlantic it aquires the 'bowtie' label and nameplate 'Chevrolet Indy V8'. In 1992 Al Unser Jr started 16 races and finished them, a reliability record unbeaten that year. He won the Indy 500 and was a consistent contender for victory, but finished the season in 3rd place. The Ilmor engines for 1993 were, of course, lighter and more powerful. (Dan R Boyd/Galmer)

IndyCar drivers tend to be competitive for a far longer period of time than those in Formula One, as can be seen from the chart below.

DRIVER	NUMBER OF SEASONS	NUMBER OF STARTS
A J FOYT	36	367
MARIO ANDRETTI	30	375
AL UNSER	30	320
J RUTHERFORD	30	315
GARY BETTENHAUSEN	28	180
GORDON JOHNCOCK	26	261
TOM SNEVA	21	205
PANCHO CARTER	20	165
RICK MEARS	18	203
TONY BETTENHAUSEN	15	102
SCOTT BRAYTON	13	130
KEVIN COGAN	12	114
BOBBY RAHAL	12	165
AL UNSER Jr	12	156
MICHAEL ANDRETTI	11	145
DANNY SULLIVAN	11	143
EMERSON FITTIPALDI	10	135
ARIE LUYENDYK	10	108
ROBERTO GUERRERO	10	104
RANDY LEWIS	9	81
DEREK DALY	9	66
JIM CRAWFORD	9	17
RAUL BOESEL	8	88
JEFF WOOD	8	37
JOHN ANDRETTI	7	71
DIDIER THEYS	7	45
SCOTT GOODYEAR	6	58
JOHN JONES	5	41
SCOTT PRUETT	5	51
EDDIE CHEEVER	5	50
JON BEEKHUIS	5	12
GUIDO DACCO	4	22
HIRO MATSSHITA	4	35
MICHAEL GROFF	4	31
WILLY T RIBBS	4	17
DEAN HALL	3	16
BUDDY LAZIER	4	30
DENNIS VITOLO	4	9
JEFF ANDRETTI	2	18
TED PRAPPAS	3	26
PAUL TRACY	3	15

Above right

Safety crews are on the scene of any incident within seconds – often before the car involved has come to a stand still. The trucks are stationed at each track and respond independently or under the direction of the chief steward. These rapid response vehicles, dubbed Safety One and Safety Two, have now been replaced with four-door crew GMCs staffed by a doctor, a paramedic and at least two rescu/extrication specialists. Each vehicle has on board a full range of firefighting, medical and special cutting tools able to deal with carbon fibre materials. (Duane J Appleget)

Right

Hey mister, your engine's on fire! Al Unser pulls off the track under the direction of the already attendant direction of Safety One during the 1990 Indy 500. (Duane J Appleget)

Speed has always been a major factor in IndyCar racing and during the past 10 years speeds have risen to over 230 mph. With such high speeds race averages have risen accordingly but to date the race average has yet to break the 190 mph barrier. The closesest challenge came from Al Unser Jr in the Michigan 500 race in 1990 when he had to fight off Bobby Rahal, going on to win the fastest IndyCar race to date.

FASTEST RACE WINNER OF THE PAST DECADE

DRIVER	YEAR	RACE	SPEED IN MPH
AL UNSER JR	1990	MICHIGAN 500	189.727
ARIE LUYENDYK	1990	INDIANAPOLIS 500	185.981
RICK MEARS	1983	MICHIGAN 200	182.325
BOBBY RAHAL	1986	MICHIGAN 250	181.701
DANNY SULLIVAN	1988	MICHIGAN 500	180.654
SCOTT GOODYEAR	1992	MICHIGAN 500	177.625
RICK MEARS	1991	INDIANAPOLIS 500	176.457
MICHAEL ANDRETTI	1987	MICHIGAN 500	171.493
BOBBY RAHAL	1986	INDIANAPOLIS 500	170.722
DANNY SULLIVAN	1989	POCONO 500	170.720

With the addition of street circuits to the IndyCar racing calendar the most noticeable effect was that the winning race average speeds fell below 70 mph. The fastest winner of the decade, Al Unser Jr, also holds the dubious honour of winning the slowest IndyCar race.

DRIVER	YEAR	RACE	SPEED IN MPH
AL UNSER Jr	1991	DENVER GP	69.576
AL UNSER Jr	1990	DENVER GP	71.243
AL UNSER Jr	1990	VANCOUVER	77.346
EMERSON FITTIPALDI	1992	AUSTRALIA	77.562
EMERSON FITTIPALDI	1991	DETROIT GP	78.824
MARIO ANDRETTI	1984	MEADOWLANDS	80.742
MICHAEL ANDRETTI	1986	LONG BEACH GP	80.965
AL UNSER Jr	1991	LONG BEACH GP	81.195
BOBBY RAHAL	1991	MEADOWLANDS	81.906
JOHN ANDRETTI	1991	AUSTRALIA	81.953

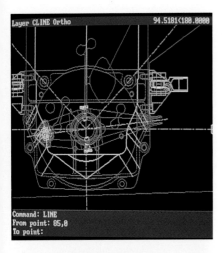

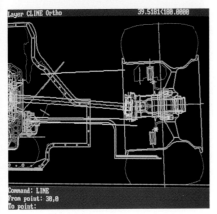

GALMER G9200 TECHNICAL SPECIFICATION

CONSTRUCTOR	Galmer Engineering
CHASSIS TYPE	G9200
WEIGHT (EMPTY)	1550 lbs
WEIGHT BIAS	Front/Rear 45%/55%
CHASSIS	Aluminium honeycomb with carbon skin
TRACK	Front 78.5" Rear 80.5"
WHEELBASE	111.0 inches
LENGTH	185 inches
FUEL CAPACITY	40 US gallons
STEERING	Rack and pinion
FRONT SUSPENSION	Push rod, Upper rocker, Inboard springs and damper.
REAR SUSPENSION	Push rod, upper rocker, Inboard springs and damper
WHEELS	Dymag magnesium
FRONT WHEEL	15" diameter 10" wide
REAR WHEEL	15" diameter 14" wide
TYRES	Goodyear Racing Eagle Radials
FRONT	25.5" diameter 10.75" wide
REAR	27.0" diameter 15.00" wide
BRAKES	Alcon Ltd, England
PAINT	PPG, USA

AERODYNAMICS

DOWNFORCE SPEEDWAY	2500 lbs plus at 200 mph
DOWNFORCE ROAD RACE	5000 lbs plus at 200 mph
ENGINE	Chevrolet Indy V8A/B
CONSTRUCTOR	Ilmor Engineering Ltd, Northampton, England
ENGINE TYPE	90° V8 aluminium block and heads
BORE & STROKE	88.0 mm × 54.4 mm
DISPLACEMENT	2647 cc (161.5 cubic inches)
COMPRESSION RATIO	11:1
FUEL SYSTEM	Ilmor Engineering electronic fuel injection
VALVE GEAR	Gear driven DOHC; 4 valves per cylinder
HORSEPOWER	720 bhp plus at 12,000 rpm
WEIGHT	325 lbs
DESIGNER	Mario Illien and Paul Morgan
FUEL	Methanol
OIL	Valvoline
ONBOARD COMPUTER	PI Electronics Ltd, England

Above

Unlike F1 cars, IndyCars are restricted to ferrous alloy iron brake discs, as shown here. For 500 mile events carbon brake rotors are allowed due to the higher speeds and subsequent high temperatures imposed upon the braking system. Strict regulations govern the specification of race car braking systems (eg, the minimum diameter of the rotor, which must be not less than eleven inches), but there is no restriction as to pad friction material

Right

Al Unser Jr prepares for the start of the Champion Spark Plug 300 at Monterey, California, 1991. The quick release steering wheel is on the screen to allow him into the car. He finished the race 2nd place behind Championship winner Michael Andretti

One of the most exciting things about IndyCar racing is the number of close finishes. Drivers who have been racing at high speeds for up to 500 miles are sometimes separated by mere fractions of a second.

DATE	EVENT/DISTANCE	MARGIN	DRIVER
10/4/21	BEVERLY HILLS 250	.02 Seconds	RALPH DE PALMA
10/4/21	BEVERLY HILLS 250	.04 Seconds	JIMMY MURPHY
25/2/23	BEVERLY HILLS 250	.05 Seconds	JIMMY MURPHY
15/6/86	PORTLAND 200	.07 Seconds	MARIO ANDRETTI

500 MILE RACES 1911-1992

24/5/92	INDIANAPOLIS 500	.04 Seconds	AL UNSER JR
30/5/82	INDIANAPOLIS 500	.16 Seconds	GORDON JOHNCOCK
04/9/15	MINNEAPOLIS 500	.25 Seconds	EARL COOPER
19/8/84	POCONO 500	.27 Seconds	DANNY SULLIVAN
28/7/85	MICHIGAN 500	.40 Seconds	EMERSON FITTIPALDI
10/3/74	ONTARIO 500	.58 Seconds	BOBBY UNSER

ROAD COURSE RACES

15/6/86	PORTLAND 200	.07 Seconds	MARIO ANDRETTI
16/5/91	DETROIT 155	.29 Seconds	EMERSON FITTIPALDI
06/4/86	LONG BEACH 158	.38 Seconds	MICHAEL ANDRETTI
03/8/80	WATKINS GLEN 150	.45 Seconds	BOBBY UNSER

An A to Z of IndyCar

AERODYNAMICS
To allow cars to travel as fast as possible great attention is centred upon its aerodynamics, how the air moves over, around and under the car as it moves through the air.

BALACLAVA
One of the biggest dangers to both the driver and the members of the crew is the potential hazard of fire. As methanol burns with a non-luminous (clear) flame in daylight, fire is difficult to spot. To protect themselves the drivers and some of the pit crew wear fire-proof clothing and hoods.

BALLOON FOOT
An uncomplimentary term for a slower driver.

BANKING
The corners of oval tracks are usually sloped or banked to allow higher speeds. The degree of banking is measured from the inside of the track to the outside wall, for example at Wisconsin State Fair Park the turns are banked at nine degrees.

BLEND LINE
The line marking identifying the entrance and exit of the pit lane from the race track.

BOOST
The manifold intake pressure above actual ambient atmospheric pressure can be increased or decreased by the driver according to the demands of the race. Increasing the boost gives more power but uses more fuel so its use is carefully monitored by the driver and team technicians. Boost is measured in inches of mercury.

BRAKE HORSE POWER (BHP)
The power output of an engine may be expressed as a Brake Horse Power which is formulated from the engine torque measured on a dynamometer. The two most common standards of presenting bhp are the SAE rating as used in the UK and in the States or DIN which is a metric rating. The two systems of rating are not equable.

CART
Championship Auto Racing Teams, Inc – the governing body of the IndyCar race series – was founded in 1978 by Roger Penske and U E 'Pat' Patrick. It is a highly efficient organisation that oversees all aspects of the racing from driver rules, safety, communications to the media and advertising rules. *CART, 390 Enterprise Court, Bloomfield Hills. MI 48302. USA.*

CATCH TANK
To prevent spillage of coolant the coolant system must incorporate a catch tank or be of a closed circuit type.

CHASSIS
The body or frame of the car to which the engine is added. Often referred to as the tub.

CHEVY
An abbreviation of the famous Chevrolet name, also known as the 'Bow-Tie marque'. It is the registered trademark of the General Motors Corporation.

CHIEF OBSERVER
The Chief Observers role is to oversee and direct the personnel responsible for observing, flags and communication around the course.

CHIEF STEWARD
The Chief Steward is the main official and representative of CART at all its events.

COVERS
To improve the aerodynamics of the wheels special lightweight covers are sometimes fitted to help reduce drag.

COMPOUND
The performance and quality of the tyres is determined by their composition or formula in manufacture. Variations in the 'recipe' will give different rates of grip, wear and running temperature which can be developed for specific race tracks.

CREW
SEE PIT CREW ASSIGNMENTS

DIRECTOR OF TIMING AND SCORING
Throughout the race the position, times and score of each and every car is the responsibility of this official and associated staff.

DIRECTOR OF SAFETY
This official has responsibility for ensuring that all safety equipment and personnel are in place before the start of the race, to supervise and direct the medical and safety crews including their equipment and to keep the Chief Steward fully aware of the safety of the race circuit.

DRAFTING
This is not a major influence as it is in other motorsports as the more aerodynamic IndyCars only make a small hole in the air. A fast moving car will create a vacuum behind it which means that a following car travelling within the vacuum is pulled along with it. The trailing car will require less effort to travel at the same speed and therefore save fuel.

DRAG (Cd)
Drag is the resistance of air to forward movement. This is measured by using a scale based upon a flat disc moving broadside through the air along its axis has a nominal Cd rating of 1.00. A typical saloon car may have a Cd of 0.36 while an IndyCar might have a Cd below 0.07.

DRY-BREAK
All the refuelling connections are of a dry-break design, which means that they do not drip allowing fuel to possibly ignite.

DYNO
The dynamometer, sometimes referred to as a 'brake', is an electronic or hydraulic device that measures the torque or power output of an engine. Based upon the rotational speed and torque figures of an engine under test the brake horsepower can be calculated.

FUEL CELL

A maximum of 40 US gallons of methanol is carried in a fuel cell made with a penetration resistant layer to meet military specifications. It is located behind the rear bulkhead of the driver's compartment and in front of the chassis/engine interface bulkhead, an area considered reasonably safe in an impact.

FUEL VALVES

All fuel valves must be clearly marked with the 'off' position.

GROUND EFFECT

The aerodynamic forces generated by the shape of the car as it passes through the air 'sucks' the car down onto the track, aiding stability and higher speeds through the turns.

HEAT EXCHANGER

Device used to lower the temperature of engine coolant through rapid heat dissipation.

HORSEPOWER

This is a unit measurement of the power output of an engine. In the United Kingdom one British horsepower equals 33,000 ft/lb of work a minute. This relates to the force needed to raise 33,000 lbs a distance of one foot in one minute, or 550 lb one foot in one second (lb/ft/sec).

IGNITION

Each car must have an ignition switch or emergency shut-off mounted within easy reach of the driver.

INDY LIGHTS

The Firestone Indy Lights Championship originated in the mid-eighties as IndyCar racing's

Above

Catch me if you can ...
Al Unser Jr exits his pit area just split seconds before team mate Danny Sullivan. (Dan R Boyd/Galmer)

only 'Official Development Program'. The exclusively Buick powered championship serves as the main training ground for future IndyCar racing drivers, team owners, mechanics, teams and other personnel.

KEVLAR

This is a brand name of a certain type of carbon fibre used in numerous ways in IndyCar racing from the drivers helmets to chassis construction to brake components.

LAPPED

When the leading cars in a race pass the slower cars at the back of the field these are then positioned 'one lap down'.

LEAD

The race lead cannot be achieved by use of the pit lane.

LINE

At each circuit there is an optimum fast way around that is quickly defined during practice or the race by the black line or 'groove' of rubber left by the cars.

MAKING THE GRID

Securing a place on the starting grid through a successful qualification run.

MANIFOLD PRESSURE RELIEF VALVE (MPRV)

This spring-loaded device is fitted to all IndyCars before the race by CART officials to ensure strict control over engine power output. The 'pop-off valve' or 'blow-off valve', set to lift if the pressure within the manifold rises above 45 inches of mercury, is fitted to the engine intake manifold. For Buick engines the manifold pressure limit is increased to 50 inches of mercury. After each practice or race the valves are collected and checked by CART officials.

MARBLES

During operation the tyres become extremely hot and soft so that fine deposits are left on the track or flung off to the side of the 'line'. These will combine with dust, grit or other fine debris left on the track surface and make the area each side of the 'line' very slippery.

MASTER SWITCH

In addition to the ignition or emergency shut-off, each car must also have a Master Switch located at the base of the rollbar on the left side of the car. The Master Switch must activate the on-board fire extinguisher and also shut off the ignition. In addition the car must also be fitted with a loop or some other device by which the switch can be operated at a distance, by a pole with a hook. This device must be clearly marked on the car with the officially supplied decal.

NOMEX

This is a brand name of the fire retardant material first developed by NASA for the early Apollo space programme in the 1960s. It is worn by most of the drivers, crew members and track officials.

OFFICIALS

All CART racing competitions must be officiated under the direction of the following approved officials:
Chief Steward
Two Stewards
Starter
Director of Timing and Scoring
Technical Chairman
Chief Observer
Registrar

ON THE BUBBLE

As soon as the grid positions are filled the slowest car is 'on the bubble' which means that it can be relegated off the grid by a faster qualifier.

OVERSTEER

A term used to describe the handling characteristics of a car. In this instance the rear of the car will tend to swing toward the outside of the track. The car is often referred to by the driver as being 'loose'. Adjustment to the suspension settings or changing the tyres usually cures the problem.

PACE CAR

When yellow flags, under which drivers must slow down and maintain their position, are displayed around the track a pace car will go out onto the track to lead the cars around at a safe pace until the track is once again clear. The pace car is a high performance model with modifications made to make it suitable for its role on the track. The high profile of IndyCar guarantees collector status for the chosen manufacturers subsequent limited edition, street legal models.

PIT

A pit area will be allocated to each competing race car with selection of order beginning with the pole car. Within the designated pit area the team must organise all of its equipment, locate its pit fuel storage tank and carry out running repairs, refuelling, etc.

PIT CREW ASSIGNMENTS

Only six members of the team are allowed on the track side of the pit wall to work on the car at any time during the race, therefore each member has a specific job, namely; Right Front (RF) – to remove and replace the right front wheel and in addition Right Rear (RR), Left Front (LF), Left Rear (LR) to carry out the appropriate action on the other wheels. The Fuel and Vent/Jack team members are responsible for refuelling the car, the vent/jack operative also raises the car with the on-board air jacks. As time is so important in each pit stop practice sessions ensure that each operation is carried out smoothly.

As an added incentive there are awards for the fastest crews at each meeting.

POLE DAY
SEE POLE POSITION

POLE POSITION

At the start of the race the fastest driver in qualifying will be the leading, pole race car on the grid. For oval tracks the pole position is on the inside of the track as determined by the first turn after the start/finish line. In road course events the pole position driver will decide whether to start from the left or the right of the track. The rest of the field will be drawn up behind in their qualifying order.

POP OFF VALVE

See manifold pressure relief valve.

PUSSY PILLOW

Many drivers use a support pad, called a 'pussy pillow' for their head during oval races to help alleviate the stresses imposed upon the neck muscles.

REGISTRAR

The registrar keeps a record of all CART members to ensure efficient administration at all events.

REVERSE

For road course events only, the transmission system must have a

reverse gear mechanism which can easily be operated by the driver.

ROOKIE
A Rookie is defined as a driver who has not competed in more than two IndyCar races in any one season or more than five in his or her career.

SET UP
To ensure that the race car is prepared to give the very best performance a mass of data is used to give the optimum handling. The crew and driver will spend all of their practice time to 'set-up' the car for the race.

SHORT CHUTE
The short straights at the northern and southern ends of the Indianapolis Motor Speedway between Turns 1 and 2 and Turns 3 and 4.

SHUNT
A collision.

SIDEPOD
The 'side pods' of the race car serve to protect the driver from side impacts and also to house the

Above
Pace car of the 1992 Indy 500, the Cadillac Allante. The cars performed all pace car duties at the Speedway in stock configuration without any modifications to the powertrain or chassis. The cars were fitted with a safety roll-bar, strobe lighting and onboard fire safety equipment. Powered by a 320 bhp Northstar V8 engine, the Allante can reach 60 mph in under seven seconds and is capable of around 150 mph. Three-time Indy 500 winner Bobby Unser was chosen by Cadillac to drive the 1993 Allante pace car for the 76th annual Indianapolis 500. Remote cameras mounted inside and outside the Caddy gave TV viewers the opportunity to ride with Unser and see the the start of the race as he commentated his way around the famous oval. (Cadillac)

radiators, the oil coolers and the computerised electronic engine management system.

SPLASH AND DASH
This is the term given to a pit stop, usually during the latter stages, made for fuel before racing hard for the end of the race.

STAGGER
To help the handling of the car at oval events it is standard procedure to run slightly larger circumference tyres on the off-side or right-hand side to help stabilise the car through the high speed turns. The difference is minimal and in road events zero stagger will be used whereby all four tyres will be exactly the same in size.

STARTER
The starter is directly responsible to the Chief Steward for carrying out the role of bringing the race cars to the start line in the correct order before starting the race and before any re-start. They are also responsible for giving any signals required during the race, either flag or lights.

STEWARDS
The two stewards act according to the directions of the Chief Steward.

SURFACE CONTACT BLOCKS
As many as six rigid plates may be added to the underside of the chassis to reduce damage caused by bottoming.

TIMING
With around 33 cars racing and continually jostling around the track it often took up to 12 hours after a race to check the timings and give the official result. Today that official result can be achieved by the USAC timekeepers and scorers quickly and more accurately thanks to computer technology.

Each car is fitted with an individually tuned, self powered small transmitter, about the size of a king size pack of cigarettes. One of these units will be supplied by an USAC official before qualifying sessions or a race and mounted on the floor of the left side pod. A series of sensors embedded in the track will register every car each time it passes over this 'time-line' and send a signal to the trackside recording computer (TRC). This records all the data of the race or qualifying period but also passes a signal to a master collating computer which feeds the USAC timing and scoring computer with each car's number, speed, lap, etc. Simple but very effective in letting everyone know the exact position and status of every car in the race.

TUB
The 'tub' or chassis is a complex structure of composite material components designed to harness the engine and protect the driver.

TURBOCHARGER
A type of engine supercharger where the exhaust gases are used to turn a compressor that force feeds air into the intake manifold.

TURBULENCE
As the car cuts through the air it creates a swirling air mass behind it which can reduce the stability of following vehicles.

UNDERSTEER
A description of the car's handling characteristics where it tends to 'push out' or run wide in the turns or bends. Fine adjustments to the wings, tyres or suspension or a combination of these will reduce the tendency.

USAC
The acronym for the United States Auto Club.

WALL
The pit/race track wall marks the operational boundary of the race track and a maximum of six team members only, excluding the driver, are allowed over this wall during a race event. The only exception to this rule is if otherwise specified by the stewards.

Below
The mandatory remote cut-out switch on Nigel Mansell's 'Red 5', highlighted by the PPG logo